To: My dear friend and Confidant
Mary Kay

You have made known to me the ways of life
O Lord;
    you will make me full of gladness with
your presence.

ACTS 2:28

From: Kay Johnson
                March 6, 2007

God's Words of Life for Catholic Women: from the Catholic Women's Devotional Bible
Copyright © 2004 by The Zondervan Corporation
ISBN 0-310-80416-7

Excerpts taken from: *Catholic Women's Devotional Bible, New Revised Standard Version.* Copyright ©2000 by The Zondervan Corporation.

All Scripture quotations, unless otherwise noted, are taken from the *New Revised Standard Version Bible: Catholic Edition.* Copyright ©1989 by the Division of Christian Education of the National Council of the Churches of Christ in the United States of America. All Rights Reserved.

Requests for information should be addressed to:
Inspirio, The gift group of Zondervan
Grand Rapids, Michigan 49530
http://www.inspiriogifts.com

Compiler: Doris Rikkers
Project Manager: Tom Dean
Design: Gayle Raymer Design
Design Manager: Val Buick

Printed in China
04 05 06/HK/ 4 3 2 1

God's Words *of* Life

for

Catholic

Women

from the
Catholic Women's Devotional Bible

NEW REVISED STANDARD VERSION

Ϋ

inspirio™

Contents

*A*chievement

I make it my ambition to proclaim the good news, not where Christ has already been named, so that I do not build on someone else's foundation.

ROMANS 15:20

Lead a life worthy of the calling to which you have been called.

EPHESIANS 4:1

If [my story] is well told and to the point, that is what I myself desired; if it is poorly done and mediocre, that was the best I could do.

2 MACCABEES 15:38

There is great gain in godliness combined with contentment.

1 TIMOTHY 6:6

God is not unjust; he will not overlook your work and the love that you showed for his sake in serving the saints, as you still do. And we want each one of you to show the same diligence so as to realize the full assurance of hope to the very end.

HEBREWS 6:10–11

*A*chievement

Hezekiah did what was good and right and faithful
before the LORD his God. And every work that he
undertook in the service of the house of God, in
accordance with the law and the commandments,
to seek his God, he did with all his heart; and
he prospered.

2 CHRONICLES 31:20–21

Commit your work to the LORD,
    and your plans will be established.

PROVERBS 16:3

Whatever your hand finds to do, do with your might.

ECCLESIASTES 9:10

The fruit of good labors is renowned,
    and the root of understanding does not fail.

THE WISDOM OF SOLOMON 3:15

Jesus said, "The slave with the two talents came
forward, saying, 'Master, you handed over to me two
talents; see, I have made two more talents.' His master
said to him, 'Well done, good and trustworthy slave;
you have been trustworthy in a few things, I will put
you in charge of many things; enter into the joy of
your master.'"

MATTHEW 25:22–23

*A*chievement

You must make very effort to support your faith with goodness, and goodness with knowledge, and knowledge with self-control, and self-control with endurance, and endurance with godliness, and godliness with mutual affection, and mutual affection with love. For if these things are yours and are increasing among you, they keep you from being ineffective and unfruitful in the knowledge of our Lord Jesus Christ. ... Therefore, brothers and sisters, be all the more eager to confirm your call and election, for if you do this, you will never stumble. For in this way; entry into the eternal kingdom of our Lord and Savior Jesus Christ will be richly provided for you.

2 PETER 1:5–8, 10–11

Jesus said, "Those who find their life will lose it, and those who lose their life for my sake will find it."

MATTHEW 10:39

I have a hope in God—a hope that they themselves also accept—that there will be a resurrection of both the righteous and the unrighteous. Therefore I do my best always to have a clear conscience toward God and all people.

ACTS 24:15–16

Jesus said, "To all those who have, more will be given, and they will have an abundance."

MATTHEW 25:29

*T*oday we are not content with little achievements, with small beginnings. We should look to Saint Theresa, the Little Flower, to walk her little way, her way of love. We should look to Saint Teresa of Avila, who was not content to be like those people who proceeded with the pace of hens about God's business, but like those people who on their own account were greatly daring in what they wished to do for God. It is we ourselves that we have to think about, no one else. That is the way the saints worked. They paid attention to what they were doing, and if others were attracted to them by their enterprise, why, well and good. But they looked to themselves first of all

After all, God is with us. It shows too much conceit to trust ourselves, to be discouraged at what we ourselves can accomplish. It is lacking in faith in God to be discouraged. After all, we are going to proceed with his help. We offer him what we are going to do. If he wishes it to prosper, it will. We must depend solely on him. Work as though everything depended on ourselves, and pray as though everything depended on God.

Dorothy Day

Angels

Because you have made the LORD your refuge,
　　the Most High your dwelling place,
no evil shall befall you,
　　no scourge come near your tent.
For he will command his angels concerning you
　　to guard you in all your ways.
On their hands they will bear you up,
　　so that you will not dash your foot against a stone.

PSALM 91:9–12

Tobit and his son kept blessing God and singing his praises, and they acknowledged God for these marvelous deeds of his when an angel of God had appeared to them.

TOBIT 12:22

The angel of the LORD encamps
　　around those who fear him and delivers them.
O taste and see that the Lord is good;
　　happy are those who take refuge in him.

PSALM 34:7–8

Daniel then said to the king, "O king, live forever! My God sent his angel and shut the lions' mouths so that they would not hurt me, because I was found blameless before him; and also before you, O king, I have done no wrong."

DANIEL 6:21–22

Angels

I saw another angel flying in mid-heaven, with an eternal gospel to proclaim to those who live on the earth—to every nation and tribe and language and people. He said in a loud voice, "Fear God and give him glory, for the hour of his judgement has come; and worship him who made heaven and earth, the sea and the springs of water."

REVELATION 14:6–7

All who sat in the council looked intently at Stephen, and they saw that his face was like the face of an angel.

ACTS 6:15

In that region there were shepherds living in the fields, keeping watch over their flock by night. Then an angel of the Lord stood before them, and the glory of the Lord shone around them, and they were terrified. But the angel said to them, "Do not be afraid, for see—I am bringing you good news of great joy for all the people: to you is born this day in the city of David a Savior, who is the Messiah, the Lord. This will be a sign for you: you will find a child wrapped in bands of cloth and lying in a manger." And suddenly there was with the angel a multitude of the heavenly host, praising God.

LUKE 2:8–13

Angels

Abraham reached out his hand and took the knife to kill his son. But the angel of the Lord called to him from heaven, and said, "Abraham, Abraham!" And he said, "Here I am." He said, "Do not lay your hand on the boy or do anything to him; for now I know that you fear God, since you have not withheld your son, your only son, from me."

GENESIS 22:10–12

Jesus knelt down, and prayed, "Father, if you are willing, remove this cup from me; yet, not my will but yours be done." Then an angel from heaven appeared to him and gave him strength.

LUKE 22:41–43

Do not neglect to show hospitality to strangers, for by doing that some have entertained angels without knowing it.

HEBREWS 13:2

The LORD has established his throne in the heavens,
    and his kingdom rules over all.
Bless the LORD, O you his angels,
    you mighty ones who do his bidding,
    obedient to his spoken word.

PSALM 103:19–20

Angels

Jesus called a child, whom he put among the disciples, and said, ... "Take care that you do not despise one of these little ones, for, I tell you, in heaven their angels continually see the face of my Father in heaven."

In the sixth month the angel Gabriel was sent by God to a town in Galilee called Nazareth, to a virgin engaged to a man whose name was Joseph of the house of David. The virgin's name was Mary. And he came to her and said, "Greetings, favored one! The Lord is with you." But she was much perplexed by his words and pondered what sort of greeting this might be. The angel said to her, "Do not be afraid, Mary, for you have found favor with God. And now, you will conceive in your womb and bear a son, and you will name him Jesus. He will be great, and will be called the Son of the Most High, and the Lord God will give to him the throne of his ancestor David. He will reign over the house of Jacob forever, and of his kingdom there will be no end." Mary said to the angel, "How can this be since I am a virgin?" The angel said to her, "The Holy Spirit will come upon you, and the power of the Most High will overshadow you; therefore the child to be born will be holy; he will be called Son of God. ... For nothing will be impossible with God." Then Mary said, "Here am I, the servant of the Lord; let it be with me according to your word." Then the angel departed from her.

LUKE 1:26–35, 37–38

Angels

God said, "My angel is with you and he is watching over your lives."

BARUCH 6:7

Christ is the reflection of God's glory and the exact imprint of God's very being, and he sustains all things by his powerful word. When he had made purification for sins, he sat down at the right hand of the Majesty on high, having become as much superior to angels as the name he has inherited is more excellent than theirs.

HEBREWS 1:3–4

I looked, and I heard the voice of many angels surrounding the throne and the living creatures and the elders; they numbered myriads of myriads and thousands of thousands, singing with full voice, "Worthy is the Lamb that was slaughtered to receive power and wealth and wisdom and might and honor and glory and blessings!"

REVELATION 5:11–12

Jesus was led up by the Spirit into the wilderness to be tempted by the devil. He fasted forty days and forty nights, and afterwards he was famished. . . . Then the devil left him, and suddenly angels came and waited on him.

MATTHEW 4:1–2,11

I believe in angels; guardian angels; the angels who came to Gideon and told a shy, not very brave young man that he was a man of valour who was going to free his people; the angels who came to Jesus in the agony of the Garden. And, what is less comforting, avenging angels, destroying angels, angels who come bringing terror when any part of God's creation becomes too rebellious, too full of pride to remember that they are God's creatures. And, most fearful of all, fallen angels, angels who have left God and followed Lucifer, and daily offer us their seductive and reasonable temptations. If we read the Bible, and if what we read has anything to do with what we believe, then we have no choice but to take angels seriously; and most artists do, from Milton to Dore to Shakespeare.

Madeleine L'Engle

*A*nxiety

Cast all your anxiety on him, because he cares for you.
1 PETER 5:7

*No one shall be able to stand against you all the days
of your life. As I was with Moses, so I will be with
you; I will not fail you or forsake you. Be strong and
courageous.*

JOSHUA 1:5–6

*We can say with confidence,
    "The Lord is my helper;
    I will not be afraid.
    What can anyone do to me?"*

HEBREWS 13:6

*God did not give us a spirit of cowardice, but rather a
spirit of power and of love and of self-discipline.*

2 TIMOTHY 1:7

I want you to be free from anxieties.

1 CORINTHIANS 7:32

Anxiety

Blessed are those who trust in the LORD,
    whose trust is the LORD.
They shall be like a tree planted by water,
    sending out its roots by the stream.
It shall not fear when heat comes,
    and its leaves shall stay green;
in the year of drought it is not anxious
    and it does not cease to bear fruit.

JEREMIAH 17:7–8

Banish anxiety from your mind, and put away pain from your body.

ECCLESIASTES 11:10

Jesus said to his disciples, 'Therefore I tell you, do not worry about your life, what you will eat, or about your body, what you will wear. For life is more than food, and the body more than clothing.'

LUKE 12:22–23

Do not worry about anything, but in everything by prayer and supplication with thanksgiving let your requests be made known to God.

PHILIPPIANS 4:6

Jealousy and anger shorten life,
    and anxiety brings on premature old age.

SIRACH 30:24

Anxiety

*Can any of you by worrying add a single hour to your
span of life? If then you are not able to do so small a
thing as that, why do you worry about the rest?*

LUKE 12:26

Do not fear, for I am with you,
  do not be afraid, for I am your God;
I will strengthen you, I will help you,
  I will uphold you with my victorious right hand.

ISAIAH 41:10

I sought the LORD, and he answered me,
  and delivered me from all my fears.
Look to him, and be radiant;
  so your faces shall never be ashamed.

PSALM 34:4–5

Anxiety weighs down the human heart,
  but a good word cheers it up.

PROVERBS 12:25

If you sit down, you will not be afraid;
  when you lie down, your sleep will be sweet.
Do not be afraid of sudden panic,
  or of the storm that strikes the wicked;
for the LORD will be your confidence
  and will keep your foot from being caught.

PROVERBS 3:24–26

Anxiety

Cast your burden on the LORD,
    and he will sustain you;
he will never permit
    the righteous to be moved.

PSALM 55:22

When I thought, 'My foot is slipping',
    your steadfast love, O LORD, held me up.
When the cares of my heart are many,
    your consolations cheer my soul.

PSALM 94:18–19

O Most High, when I am afraid,
    I put my trust in you.
In God, whose word I praise,
    in God I trust; I am not afraid;
    what can flesh do to me?

PSALM 56:2–4

Be still and know that I am God!
    I am exalted among the nations,
    I am exalted in the earth.
The LORD of hosts is with us;
    the God of Jacob is our refuge.

PSALM 46:10–11

*A*nxiety

But for me it is good to be near God;
    I have made the Lord GOD my refuge,
    to tell of all your works.

PSALM 73:28

Blessed be the LORD,
    who daily bears us up;
    God is our salvation.

PSALM 68:19

One Sunday evening, I made the mistake of rehearsing the week ahead. All my anxieties about work came flooding in. I shut my eyes and prayed, admitting that I didn't know what to do and asking God's help.

I dreamed I had agreed to fill in as a last-minute speaker at a women's luncheon at a local church. As soon as I said yes, I panicked: with only twenty minutes to prepare, I hadn't the slightest idea what I would say. I took off running and soon found myself sprinting across the top of a piano. As I glanced down, I noticed a piece of sheet music, entitled "Be Still, and Know that I Am God." Suddenly, it dawned on me—I had been given the text of my talk! As the luncheon was about to begin, I woke up.

When I opened my eyes, I realized that the message was meant for me, not for the women in my dream. God was trying to get through to me about my own anxiety. I was running too fast, doing too much, trying to take charge of things that were outside my control. I needed to stop saying yes to the impossible demands I placed on myself to slow down and learn to be still, letting God be God in every situation in my life.

Ann Spangler

Attitude

Rejoice in the Lord always; again I will say, Rejoice. Let your gentleness be known to everyone. The Lord is near.

PHILIPPIANS 4:4–5

I heard the voice of the Lord saying, 'Whom shall I send, and who will go for us?' And I said, 'Here am I; send me!'

ISAIAH 6:8

Set your minds on things that are above, not on things that are on earth, for you have died, and your life is hidden with Christ in God. When Christ who is your life is revealed, then you also will be revealed with him in glory.

COLOSSIANS 3:2–4

Jesus said, "In everything do to others as you would have them do to you; for this is the law and the prophets."

MATTHEW 7:12

Whether you eat or drink, or whatever you do, do everything for the glory of God. Give no offense to Jews or to Greeks or to the church of God, just as I try to please everyone in everything I do, not seeking my own advantage, but that of many, so that they may be saved.

1 CORINTHIANS 10:31–33

Attitude

Do not lag in zeal, be ardent in spirit, serve the Lord.

ROMANS 12:11

What does the LORD require of you
but to do justice, and to love kindness,
and to walk humbly with your God?

MICAH 6:8

*Let each of you look not to your own interests, but to
the interest of others.*

PHILIPPIANS 2:4

*Whoever wishes to become great among you must be
your servant, and whoever wishes to be first among
you must be slave of all. For the Son of Man came not
to be served but to serve, and to give his life a ransom
for many.*

MARK 10:43–45

*By the grace given to me I say to everyone among you
not to think of yourself more highly than you ought to
think, but to think with sober judgment, each according
to the measure of faith that God has assigned.*

ROMANS 12:3

*Beloved, whatever is true, whatever is honorable,
whatever is just, whatever is pure, whatever is
pleasing, whatever is commendable, if there is any
excellence and if there is anything worthy of praise,
think about these things.*

PHILIPPIANS 4:8

Attitude

As for you, man of God, ... pursue righteousness, godliness, faith, love, endurance, gentleness.

1 Timothy 6:11

Let the word of Christ dwell in you richly; teach and admonish one another in all wisdom; and with gratitude in your hearts sing psalms, hymns, and spiritual songs to God. And whatever you do, in word or deed, do everything in the name of the Lord Jesus, giving thanks to God the Father through him.

Colossians 3:16–17

All of you must clothe yourselves with humility in your dealings with one another, for
> "God opposes the proud,
> but gives grace to the humble."

1 Peter 5:5

Let the same mind be in you that was in Christ Jesus,
who, though he was in the form of God,
> did not regard equality with God
> as something to be exploited,
but emptied himself,
> taking the form of a slave,
> being born in human likeness,
And being found in human form,
> he humbled himself
> and became obedient to the point of death—
> even death on a cross.

Philippians 2:5–8

*D*uring Dante's vision of heaven in the Paradiso, he describes the universe-size rose of souls that surrounds the divine throne with utter beauty. He wonders aloud to a soul on the edge of this rose, farthest from the throne, whether he is content there. The soul replies that he so loves God he is thrilled to be in whatever place God has put him; he is filled with God's praise and God's love—how can he wish for more?

It is a rare person who loves enough to rejoice in all goodness, whether he or she benefits directly or not. Yet we can all practice this happy attitude. When we hear of something wonderful falling into another's life, we can set aside that nagging "But what about me?" and simply enjoy the beauty with that person. We may even celebrate it. It is recommended that we do this, even though in the beginning it may feel unreal, if we have habitually envied every good thing that happened to others. Our emotions carry on in their habits, but do our emotions tell us the truth? Rarely!

Marilyn Gustin

Blessing

All these blessings shall come upon you and overtake you, if you obey the LORD your God.

DEUTERONOMY 28:2

Blessed shall you be when you come in, and blessed shall you be when you go out.

DEUTERONOMY 28:6

You bless the righteous, O LORD;
 you cover them with favor as with a shield.

PSALM 5:12

May God do good to you, and may he remember his covenant with Abraham and Isaac and Jacob, his faithful servants. May he give you all a heart to worship him and to do his will with a strong heart and a willing spirit. May he open your heart to his law and his commandments, and may he bring peace. May he hear your prayers and be reconciled to you, and may he not forsake you in time of evil.

2 MACCABEES 1:2–5

May the Lord give you increase,
 both you and your children.
May you be blessed by the LORD,
 who made heaven and earth.

PSALM 115:14–15

*B*lessing

The blessing of the Lord is the reward of the pious,
    and quickly God causes his blessing to flourish.

SIRACH 11:22

*The LORD will command the blessing upon you in
your barns, and in all that you undertake; he will
bless you in the land that the LORD your God is
giving you. The LORD will establish you as his holy
people, as he has sworn to you, if you keep the
commandments of the LORD your God and walk in
his ways.*

DEUTERONOMY 28:8–9

[God] lifts up the soul and makes the eyes sparkle;
    he gives health and life and blessing.

SIRACH 34:20

*I will make [my people] and the region around my
hill a blessing; and I will send down the showers in
their season, they shall be showers of blessing. ... You
are my sheep, the sheep of my pasture, and I am your
God, says the Lord GOD.*

EZEKIEL 34:26,31

May mercy, peace, and love be yours in abundance.

JUDE 2

*B*lessing

Jesus said, "Blessed are the poor in spirit, for theirs is the kingdom of heaven.
Blessed are those who mourn, for they will be comforted.
Blessed are the meek, for they will inherit the earth.
Blessed are those who hunger and thirst for righteousness, for they will be filled.
Blessed are the merciful, for they will receive mercy.
Blessed are the pure in heart, for they will see God.
Blessed are the peacemakers, for they will be called children of God.
Blessed are those who are persecuted for righteousness' sake, for theirs is the kingdom of heaven."

MATTHEW 5:3–10

The same Lord is Lord of all and is generous to all who call on him.

ROMANS 10:12

Though I am free with respect to all, I have made myself a slave to all, so that I might win more of them. ... I do it all for the sake of the gospel, so that I may share in its blessings.

1 CORINTHIANS 9:19,23

Blessed be the God and Father of our Lord Jesus Christ, who has blessed us in Christ with every spiritual blessing in the heavenly places, just as he chose us in Christ before the foundation of the world to be holy and blameless before him in love.

EPHESIANS 1:3–4

*B*lessing

Blessed is anyone who endures temptation. Such a one has stood the test and will receive the crown of life that the Lord has promised to those who love him.

JAMES 1:12

The LORD bless you and keep you;
   the LORD make his face to shine upon you, and
   be gracious to you;
   the LORD lift up his countenance upon you, and
   give you peace.

NUMBERS 6:24–26

Blessed is the one who reads aloud the words of the prophecy, and blessed are those who hear and who keep what is written in it; for the time is near.

REVELATION 1:3

Happy is everyone who fears the LORD,
   who walks in his ways.
You shall eat the fruit of the labor of your hands;
   you shall be happy, and it shall go well with you.

PSALM 128:1–2

Blessings are on the head of the righteous,
   but the mouth of the wicked conceals violence.

PROVERBS 10:6

May the LORD, maker of heaven and earth,
   bless you from Zion.

PSALM 134:3

*B*lessing

Jesus said. "Blessed are you when people revile you and persecute you and utter all kinds of evil against you falsely on my account. Rejoice and be glad, for your reward is great in heaven, for in the same way they persecuted the prophets who were before you."

MATTHEW 5:11–12

Even if you do suffer for doing what is right, you are blessed. Do not fear what they fear, and do not be intimidated, but in your hearts sanctify Christ as Lord. Always be ready to make your defense to anyone who demands from you an account of the hope that is in you.

1 PETER 3:14–15

Bring the full tithe into the storehouse, so that there may be food in my house, and thus put me to the test, says the LORD of hosts; see if I will not open the windows of heaven for you and pour down for you an overflowing blessing.

MALACHI 3:10

Happy are the people to whom such blessings fall;
     happy are the people whose God is the LORD.

PSALM 144:15

Special blessings are a part of Catholic life. They are holy words through which God enters our everyday world and helps us use his gifts in the spirit of the gospel. All blessings are "let it happen" statements that originate with God and are spoken on his behalf. God himself pronounced the first blessings—over birds and sea creatures, Adam and Eve, Noah and his sons. He taught Aaron, Israel's first high priest to bless the people in his name. The New Testament shows Jesus blessing children, food, and followers.

Because blessings come from God, they really do something. Like a key in the ignition, they activate a special kind of power. Food is made holy, catechists are commissioned, homes and religious articles are dedicated to God's service, and animals are put under special protection.

Through the words of every blessing, we are reminded that God is the source of life and of every good thing. Even as we ask God to sanctify what we offer, we acknowledge that the offering itself is something he has blessed us with. Blessings verbalize a loving God's desire for his children's welfare. They are God's wishes made audible.

Louise Perrotta

Comfort

Thus says the LORD: ...
As a mother comforts her child,
    so I will comfort you;
    you shall be comforted in Jerusalem.

ISAIAH 66:12–13

Blessed be the God and Father of our Lord Jesus
Christ, the Father of mercies and the God of all
consolation, who consoles us in all our affliction, so
that we may be able to console those who are in any
affliction with the consolation with which we ourselves
are consoled by God.

2 CORINTHIANS 1:3–4

Blessed are those who mourn, for they will be
comforted.

MATTHEW 5:4

[Thus says the LORD:]
Listen to me, O house of Jacob,
    all the remnant of the house of Israel,
who have been borne by me from your birth,
    carried from the womb;
even to your old age I am he,
    even when you turn gray I will carry you.
I have made, and I will bear;
    I will carry and will save.

ISAIAH 46:3–4

Comfort

Comfort, O comfort my people,
    says your God.
Speak tenderly to Jerusalem
    and cry to her
that she has served her term,
    that her penalty is paid,
that she has received from the LORD'S hand
    double for all her sins.

ISAIAH 40:1–2

I am not alone because the Father is with me.

JOHN 16:32

You, O Lord, are a God merciful and gracious,
    slow to anger and abounding in steadfast love
    and faithfulness. ...
Show me a sign of your favor,
    so that those who hate me may see it and be put
    to shame,
    because you, LORD, have helped me and
    comforted me.

PSALM 86:15,17

Remember your word to your servant,
    in which you have made me hope.
This is my comfort in my distress,
    that your promise gives me life.

PSALM 119:49–50

Comfort

You who have done great things,
    O God, who is like you?
You who have made me see many troubles and calamities
    will revive me again;
from the depths of the earth
    you will bring me up again.
You will increase my honor,
    and comfort me once again.

PSALM 71:19–21

You will say on that day;
    I will give thanks to you, O LORD,
    for though you were angry with me,
your anger turned away,
    and you comforted me.

ISAIAH 12:1

A joyful heart is life itself,
    and rejoicing lengthens one's life span.
Indulge yourself and take comfort,
    and remove sorrow far from you,
for sorrow has destroyed many,
    and no advantage ever comes from it.

SIRACH 30:22–23

A mission organization printed a calendar that contained photos depicting everyday life in the mission community. One photo showed a woman working at basketmaking. Her toddler son was standing there, nursing at her breast.

The message of comfort conveyed by this image would have been easily understood and welcomed as a metaphor for God's nurturing and restorative love. The reign of God is presented here in the image of the nursing mother: "You shall nurse and be carried on her arm, and dandled on her knees. As a mother comforts her child, so I will comfort you" (Isaiah 66:12-13).

When our zeal for the task outstrips our abilities, and we collapse, like a toddler, in a tantrum of frustration, our God, like a loving Mother, scoops us up, hugs and cuddles us, and gives us the nurturing we need to be refreshed and joyful. It is in this loving relationship that the reign of God becomes fully realized. When our words fail, when our best laid plans collapse, when the fulfillment of the dream seems completely lost—God loves us, nurtures us, restores us. The reign of God becomes reality in the union of God and humanity in loving embrace.

Kathleen Spears Hopkins

Compassion

The compassion of human beings is for their neighbors,
>   but the compassion of the Lord is for every
>   living thing.
He rebukes and trains and teaches them,
>   and turns them back, as a shepherd his flock.
He has compassion on those who accept his discipline
>   and who are eager for his precepts.

SIRACH 18:13–14

Thus says the LORD of hosts: Render true judgments,
show kindness and mercy to one another; do not
oppress the widow, the orphan, the alien, or the
poor; and do not devise evil in your hearts against
one another.

ZECHARIAH 7:9–10

Indeed we call blessed those who showed endurance.
You have heard of the endurance of Job, and you have
seen the purpose of the Lord, how the Lord is
compassionate and merciful.

JAMES 5:11

Jesus said, "Give to everyone who begs from you, and
do not refuse anyone who wants to borrow from you."

MATTHEW 5:42

As a father has compassion for his children,
>   so the LORD has compassion for those you fear him

PSALM 103:13

Compassion

In overflowing wrath for a moment I hid my face
from you,
>   but with everlasting love I will have compassion
>   on you,
>   says the LORD, your redeemer.

ISAIAH 54:8

My heart recoils within me;
>   my compassion grows warm and tender.
I will not execute my fierce anger;
>   I will not again destroy Ephraim;
for I am God and no mortal,
>   the Holy One in your midst,
>   and I will not come in wrath.

HOSEA 11:8–9

The LORD, the LORD
>   a God merciful and gracious,
slow to anger, and abounding in steadfast love and
>   faithfulness,
keeping steadfast love for the thousandth generation,
>   forgiving iniquity and transgression and sin.

EXODUS 34:6–7

The mountains may depart
>   and the hills be removed,
but my steadfast love shall not depart from you,
>   and my covenant of peace shall not be removed,
>   says the LORD, who has compassion on you.

ISAIAH 54:10

Compassion

All of you, have unity of spirit, sympathy, love for one another, a tender heart, and a humble mind. Do not repay evil for evil or abuse for abuse; but on the contrary, repay with a blessing. It is for this that you were called—that you might inherit a blessing.

1 PETER 3:8–9

Those who despise their neighbors are sinners,
    but happy are those who are kind to the poor.

PROVERBS 14:21

Naomi said to her two daughters-in-law, "Go back each of you to your mother's house. May the LORD deal kindly with you, as you have dealt with the dead and with me."

RUTH 1:8

The Lord is compassionate and merciful;
    he forgives sins and saves in time of distress.

SIRACH 2:11

Jesus said, "Do to others as you would have them do to you."

LUKE 6:31

Contribute to the needs of the saints; extend hospitality to strangers.

ROMANS 12:13

Compassion

Jesus said also to the one who had invited him,
"When you give a luncheon or a dinner, do not invite
your friends or your brothers or your relatives or rich
neighbors, in case they may invite you in return, and
you would be repaid. But when you give a banquet,
invite the poor, the crippled, the lame, and the blind.
And you will be blessed, because they cannot repay
you, for you will be repaid at the resurrection of the
righteous."

LUKE 14:12–14

Is not this the fast that I choose:
     to loose the bonds of injustice,
     to undo the thongs of the yoke,
to let the oppressed go free,
     and to break every yoke?
Is it not to share your bread with the hungry,
     and bring the homeless poor into your house;
when you see the naked, to cover them,
     and not to hide yourself from your own kin?
Then your light shall break forth like the dawn,
     and your healing shall spring up quickly;
your vindicator shall go before you,
     the glory of the LORD shall be your rear guard.
Then you shall call, and the LORD will answer;
     you shall cry for help, and he will say, Here I am.

ISAIAH 58:6–8

Compassion

Jesus said, "Then the King will say ...'I was hungry and you gave me food, I was thirsty and you gave me something to drink, I was a stranger and you welcomed me, I was naked and you gave me clothing, I was sick and you took care of me, I was in prison and you visited me.' Then the righteous will answer him, 'Lord, when was it that we saw you hungry and gave you food, or thirsty and give you something to drink? And when was it that we saw you a stranger and welcomed you, or naked and gave you clothing? And when was it that we saw you sick or in prison and visited you?' And the king will answer them, 'Truly I tell you, just as you did it to one of the least of these who are members of my family, you did it to me.'"

MATTHEW 25:34–40

Be kind to one another, tenderhearted, forgiving one another, as God in Christ has forgiven you.

EPHESIANS 4:32

Bless the LORD, O my soul,
    and do not forget all his benefits—
who forgives all your iniquity,
    who heals all your diseases,
who redeems your life from the Pit,
    who crowns you with steadfast love and mercy,
who satisfies you with good as long as you live
    so that your youth is renewed like the eagle's.

PSALM 103:2–5

*W*hat a difference a really sisterly feeling among women would make!

I was reminded of an incident told me by a doctor. She does much maternity work, and one day a woman come to the clinic who expected her twelfth baby. She looked a battered wreck, dragging two small children, utterly depressed, unable to face life. The doctor suddenly remembered a very beautiful baby carriage given her by a wealthy patient. It was of a type hardly ever seen today, shining with brilliant paint and chromium, hung on springs and light to push, but with seats for two children and room for parcels besides. As the woman walked away proudly pushing her two children in it, she appeared transformed. How small a thing, the doctor said, can work a change in the outlook of the very poor.

But it was more than merely the baby carriage: This gift typified the just honor shown to her condition. It expressed the compassion of another Catholic woman: that compassion which means suffering with, bearing the burden with, those women who have the courage today to face the fullest weight that a mother can have to bear—a large family to be brought up in a city slum.

Maisie Ward

Contentment

*I have learned to be content with whatever I have. I
know what it is to have little, and I know what it is to
have plenty. In any and all circumstances I have
learned the secret of being well-fed and of going hungry,
of having plenty and of being in need.*

PHILIPPIANS 4:11–12

Be content with little or much,
and you will hear no reproach for being a guest.

SIRACH 29:23

*Of course, there is great gain in godliness combined
with contentment; for we brought nothing into the
world, so that we can take nothing out of it; but if we
have food and clothing, we will be content with these.*

1 TIMOTHY 6:6–7

Better is little with the fear of the LORD
than great treasure and trouble with it.

PROVERBS 15:16

Satisfy us, O LORD, in the morning with your steadfast love,
so that we may rejoice and be glad all our days.

PSALM 90:14

*Let each of you lead the life that the Lord has
assigned, to which God called you.*

1 CORINTHIANS 7:17

Contentment

Keep your lives free from the love of money, and be content with what you have.

Hebrews 13:5

The fear of the LORD is life indeed;
> filled with it one rests secure and suffers no harm.

Proverbs 19:23

As for me, I shall behold your face in righteousness;
> when I awake I shall be satisfied, beholding your
> likeness.

Psalm 17:15

Better is a handful with quiet
> than two handfuls with toil and a chasing after wind.

Ecclesiastes 4:6

Better is a dry morsel with quiet
> than a house full of feasting with strife.

Proverbs 17:1

The eyes of all look to you, O LORD,
> and you give them their food in due season.
You open your hand,
> satisfying the desire of every living thing.

Psalm 145:15–16

Contentment

Trust in the LORD with all your heart,
and do not rely on your own insight.
In all your ways acknowledge him,
and he will make straight your paths.

PROVERBS 3:5–6

Jesus said, "Do not store up for yourselves treasures on earth, where moth and rust consume and where thieves break in and steal; but store up for yourselves treasures in heaven, where neither moth nor rust consumes and where thieves do not break in and steal. For where your treasure is, there your heart will be also."

MATTHEW 6:19–21

I commend enjoyment, for there is nothing better for people under the sun than to eat, and drink, and enjoy themselves, for this will go with them in their toil through the days of life that God gives them under the sun.

ECCLESIASTES 8:15

Better is a little with righteousness
than large income with injustice.

PROVERBS 16:8

I sigh and look about me at last year's acquisitions—the silver bowl that didn't polish up well enough to grace the dining table but looks elegant with my English ivy growing out of it, the slightly unbalanced coat rack that stands up straight and handsome since I wedged it in the hall corner, the old washday boiler painted black that was just right to hold logs next to the fireplace.

Yes, I know. It's a madness, a craving. I should kick the habit and give up garages. But even now, in the clean white snow of winter, I long for a dark dirty garage with a sale sign on it!

Dear Lord, why do we always yearn for more? Forgive my love of shopping, my need to change things around. Maybe it's a sign, Lord, of my yearning for you. In always searching, maybe it is you I am searching for. My need to change the house may be a symbol of my inner need to change myself. My need to add to my possessions may be a result of my need to possess you more. Help me sort out my priorities, Lord. Help me empty my life a bit, so I will have more time for prayer and more room to be filled by thoughts of you.

Bernadette McCarver Snyder

Encouragement

With my voice I cry to the LORD;
  with my voice I make supplication to the LORD.
I pour out my complaint before him;
  I tell my trouble before him.
When my spirit is faint,
  you know my way.

PSALM 142:1–3

May the God of steadfastness and encouragement
grant you to live in harmony with one another, in
accordance with Christ Jesus, so that together you
may with one voice glorify the God and Father of our
Lord Jesus Christ.

ROMANS 15:5–6

I have indeed received much joy and encouragement
from your love, because the hearts of the saints have
been refreshed through you.

PHILEMON 7

I lift up my eyes to the hills—
  from where will my help come?
My help comes from the LORD,
  who made heaven and earth.
He will not let your foot be moved;
  he who keeps you will not slumber.
He who keeps Israel
  will neither slumber nor sleep.

PSALM 121:1–4

*E*ncouragement

Whatever was written in former days was written for our instruction, so that by steadfastness and by the encouragement of the scriptures we might have hope.

ROMANS 15:4

Blessed be the God and Father of our Lord Jesus Christ! By his great mercy he has given us a new birth into a living hope through the resurrection of Jesus Christ from the dead. ... In this you rejoice, even if now for a little while you have had to suffer various trials.

1 PETER 1:3,6

The LORD is my rock, my fortress, and my deliverer,
    my God, my rock in whom I take refuge,
    my shield, and the horn of my salvation, my
    stronghold.

PSALM 18:2

My brothers and sisters, whenever you face trials of any kind, consider it nothing but joy, because you know that the testing of your faith produces endurance; and let endurance have its full effect, so that you may be mature and complete, lacking in nothing.

JAMES 1:2–4

Take courage; the time is near for God to heal you; take courage.

TOBIT 5:10

Encouragement

Let me hear of your steadfast love in the morning,
     for in you I put my trust, O LORD.
Teach me the way I should go,
     for to you I lift up my soul.

PSALM 143:8

Strengthen the weak hands,
     and make firm the feeble knees.
Say to those who are of a fearful heart,
     "Be strong, do not fear!
Here is your God.
     He will come with vengeance,
with terrible recompense.
     He will come and save you."

ISAIAH 35:3–4

*Jesus answered, "I have said this to you, so that in me
you may have peace. In the world you face persecution.
But take courage; I have conquered the world!"*

JOHN 16:33

My soul continually thinks of it
     and is bowed down within me.
But this I call to mind,
     and therefore I have hope:
The steadfast love of the LORD never ceases,
     his mercies never come to an end;
they are new every morning;
     great is your faithfulness.

LAMENTATIONS 3:20–23

Encouragement

We do not lose heart. Even though our outer nature is wasting away, our inner nature is being renewed day by day. For this slight momentary affliction is preparing us for an eternal weight of glory beyond all measure, because we look not at what can be seen but at what cannot be seen, for what can be seen is temporary, but what cannot be seen is eternal.

2 CORINTHIANS 4:16–18

You, take courage! Do not let your hands be weak, for your work shall be rewarded.

2 CHRONICLES 15:7

The LORD is a stronghold for the oppressed,
    a stronghold in times of trouble.

PSALM 9:9

Let us hold fast to the confession of our hope without wavering, for he who has promised is faithful. And let us consider how to provoke one another to love and good deeds, not neglecting to meet together, as is the habit of some, but encouraging one another, and all the more as you see the Day approaching.

HEBREWS 10:23–25

The LORD is my light and my salvation;
    whom shall I fear?
The LORD is the stronghold of my life;
    of whom shall I be afraid?

PSALM 27:1

*E*ncouragement

*We urge you beloved, to admonish the idlers,
encourage the fainthearted, help the weak; be patient
with all of them.*

1 THESSALONIANS 5:14

You, O LORD, are a shield around me,
my glory, and the one who lifts up my head.
I cry aloud to the LORD,
and he answers me from his holy hill.

PSALM 3:3–4

Surely God is my helper;
the Lord is the upholder of my life.
For he has delivered me from every trouble,
and my eye has looked in triumph on my enemies.

PSALM 54:4,7

The LORD will keep you from all evil;
he will keep your life. ...
The LORD will keep
your going out and your coming in
from this time on and forevermore.

PSALM 121:7–8

*Come to me, all you that are weary and are carrying
heavy burdens, and I will give you rest. Take my yoke
upon you and learn from me; for I am gentle and
humble in heart, and you will find rest for your souls.
For my yoke is easy, and my burden is light.*

MATTHEW 11:28–30

*I*n England one afternoon we took a drive in the country. A sudden storm came up, so we pulled off the road to wait it out.

In the distance I saw a man who had a large cloak on and a shepherd's crook in his hand. He was calling his sheep. They came, bells tinkling from different parts of the field. The shepherd never moved in all that rain and lightning, but stood steady for his flock to gather round him.

That scene has been forever engraved on my memory. The shepherd didn't leave his sheep. He didn't let them find refuge of their own. But neither did he take them out of the storm. Instead he provided them with safety and security by his presence.

So God our shepherd desires to do for us. In times of crisis, in the midst of a storm, let us not try to save ourselves. Let us run quickly to the shelter of his arms, where we will find refuge, and stay there until the storm passes by.

For God knows us, and he knows all our needs. He will provide in the midst of the storm. The fruit of such faith is peace and confidence in a God who cares.

Ann Shields

Faith

Faith is the assurance of things hoped for, the conviction of things not seen. ... And without faith it is impossible to please God, for whoever would approach him must believe that he exists and that he rewards those who seek him.

HEBREWS 11:1,6

Jesus said to him, "Have you believed because you have seen me? Blessed are those who have not seen and yet have come to believe."

JOHN 20:29

If you confess with your lips that Jesus is Lord and believe in your heart that God raised him from the dead, you will be saved. For one believes with the heart and so is justified, and one confesses with the mouth and so is saved.

ROMANS 10:9–10

Look at the proud!
Their spirit is not right in them,
but the righteous live by their faith.

HABAKKUK 2:4

Faith comes from what is heard, and what is heard comes through the word of Christ.

ROMANS 10:17

$\mathcal{F}$aith

Jesus said to him, "If you are able!—All things can be done for the one who believes."

MARK 9:23

To one who without works trusts him who justifies the ungodly, such faith is reckoned as righteousness.

ROMANS 4:5

Keep alert, stand firm in your faith, be courageous, be strong. Let all that you do be done in love.

1 CORINTHIANS 16:13

It is no longer I who live, but it is Christ who lives in me. And the life I now live in the flesh I live by faith in the Son of God, who loved me and gave himself for me.

GALATIANS 2:20

As you therefore have received Christ Jesus the Lord, continue to live your lives in him, rooted and built up in him and established in the faith, just as you were taught, abounding in thanksgiving.

COLOSSIANS 2:6–7

You are being protected by the power of God through faith for a salvation ready to be revealed in the last time.

1 PETER 1:4–5

Faith

*Since we are justified by faith, we have peace with
God through our Lord Jesus Christ.*

Romans 5:1

*Jesus answered, "Have faith in God. Truly I tell you,
If you say to this mountain, 'Be taken up and thrown
into the sea,' and if you do not doubt in your heart,
but believe that what you say will come to pass, it will
be done for you. So I tell you, whatever you ask for
in prayer, believe that you have received it, and it will
be yours."*

Mark 11:22–24

*In our prayers for you we always thank God, the
Father of our Lord Jesus Christ, for we have heard of
your faith in Christ Jesus and of the love that you
have for all the saints.*

Colossians 1:3–4

*I pray that, according to the riches of God's glory, he
may grant that you may be strengthened in your
inner being with power through his Spirit, and that
Christ may dwell in your hearts, through faith, as you
are being rooted and grounded in love.*

Ephesians 3:16–17

*Abram believed the Lord; and the Lord reckoned it
to him as righteousness.*

Genesis 15:6

Faith

Whatever is born of God conquers the world. And this is the victory that conquers the world, our faith.

1 JOHN 5:4

The genuineness of your faith—being more precious than gold that, though perishable, is tested by fire— may be found to result in praise and glory and honor when Jesus Christ is revealed. Although you have not seen him, you love him, and even though you do not see him now, you believe in him and rejoice with an indescribable and glorious joy, for you are receiving the outcome of your faith, the salvation of your souls.

1 PETER 1:7–9

Believe on the Lord Jesus, and you will be saved, you and your household.

ACTS 16:31

By faith we understand that the worlds were prepared by the word of God, so that what is seen was made from things that are not visible.

HEBREWS 11:3

Jesus said to them, ... "Truly I tell you, if you have faith the size of a mustard seed, you will say to this mountain, 'Move from here to there,' and it will move; and nothing will be impossible for you."

MATTHEW 17:20–21

Faith

You must make every effort to support your faith with goodness, and goodness with knowledge, and knowledge with self-control, and self-control with endurance, and endurance with godliness, and godliness with mutual affection, and mutual affection with love. For these things are yours and are increasing among you, they keep you from being ineffective and unfruitful in the knowledge of our Lord Jesus Christ.

2 PETER 1:5–8

Jesus said, "Whatever you ask for in prayer with faith, you will receive."

MATTHEW 21:22

We walk by faith, not by sight.

2 CORINTHIANS 5:7

Jesus said, "This is indeed the will of my Father, that all who see the Son and believe in him may have eternal life; and I will raise them up on the last day."

JOHN 6:40

I am not ashamed of the gospel; it is the power of God for salvation to everyone who has faith. For in it the righteousness of God is revealed through faith for faith; as it is written, "The one who is righteous will live by faith."

ROMANS 1:16–17

We are all waiting for great opportunities to show heroism, letting countless opportunities go by to enlarge our hearts, increase our faith, and show our love for our fellows, and so for him. We are living in this world and must make choices now, choices that may mean the sacrifice of our lives in the future, but for now our goods, our reputations even.

We are trying to spread the gospel of peace. And in doing this we are accounted fools, and it is the folly of the Cross in the eyes of an unbelieving world.

Martyrdom is not [always] gallantly standing before a firing squad. Usually it is the losing of a job because of not taking a loyalty oath, or buying a war bond, or paying a tax. Martyrdom is small, hidden, misunderstood. Or if it is a bloody martyrdom, it is the cry in the dark, the terror, the shame, the loneliness, nobody to hear, nobody to suffer with, let alone to save.

But we proclaim our faith. Christ has died for us. Adam and Eve fell, and as Julian of Norwich wrote, the worst has already happened and been repaired. It is [Christ's] dying, not the killing in wars, which will save the world.

Dorothy Day

Faithfulness

Know therefore that the LORD *your God is God, the faithful God who maintains covenant loyalty with those who love him and keep his commandments, to a thousand generations.*

DEUTERONOMY 7:9

Your steadfast love, O LORD, extends to the heavens,
    your faithfulness to the clouds.

PSALM 36:5

Nehemiah said, "I gave my brother Hanani charge over Jerusalem, along with Hananiah the commander of the citadel—for he was a faithful man and feared God more than many."

NEHEMIAH 7:2

Praise the LORD, all you nations!
    Extol him, all you peoples!
For great is his steadfast love toward us,
    and the faithfulness of the LORD endures forever.
Praise the LORD!

PSALM 117:1-2

Brothers and sisters, holy partners in a heavenly calling, consider that Jesus, the apostle and high priest of our confession, was faithful to the one who appointed him, just as Moses also was faithful in all God's house.

HEBREWS 3:1

*F*aithfulness

The presidents and the satraps tried to find grounds for complaint against Daniel in connection with the kingdom. But they could find no grounds for complaint or any corruption, because he was faithful, and no negligence or corruption could be found in him.

DANIEL 6:4

The LORD is faithful in all his words,
    and gracious in all his deeds.
The LORD upholds all who are falling,
    and raises up all who are bowed down.

PSALM 145:13–14

God is faithful, and he will not let you be tested beyond your strength, but with the testing he will also provide the way out so that you may be able to endure it.

1 CORINTHIANS 10:13

The LORD is good;
    his steadfast love endures forever,
    and his faithfulness to all generations.

PSALM 100:5

Faithfulness

The LORD loves those who hate evil;
>   he guards the lives of his faithful;
>   he rescues them from the hand of the wicked.
Light dawns for the righteous,
>   and joy for the upright in heart.
Rejoice in the LORD, O you righteous,
>   and give thanks to his holy name!

PSALM 97:10–12

O LORD *God of hosts,*
>   who is as mighty as you, O LORD?
>   Your faithfulness surrounds you. ...
Righteousness and justice are the foundation of your throne;
>   steadfast love and faithfulness go before you.

PSALM 89:8,14

The faithful will abound with blessings,
>   but one who is in a hurry to be rich will not go unpunished.

PROVERBS 28:20

No one is likely to command us to kneel before a golden statue today [as in the book of Daniel]. Our culture promotes more subtle idols that demand our allegiance: sexual icons, success at any price, lust for power, unbridled materialism. The old idols keep popping up, disguised for modern times. Resisting the temptation to give in to these cultural idols often entails great personal sacrifice.

Consider the single man or woman who refuses to give in to the fires of sexual passion, or the husband or wife who resists the temptation to sacrifice family life at the altar of career, or the unmarried woman who hears the dreaded news that she's pregnant but who resists the pressure to solve the "problem" with a quick visit to the local abortion clinic.

None of these are easy choices to make. We will often suffer loss, fear, confusion, and pain in our quest to be faithful to what and whom we believe in. But as we trust God for the outcome, we will experience a new freedom. Perhaps an angel will even stand by our side in the midst of our distress, unbinding and protecting us from the devouring flames that threaten to consume us.

Ann Spangler

Family

I take pleasure in three things,
> and they are beautiful in the sight of God and of
> mortals:

agreement among brothers and sisters, friendship
among neighbors,
> and a wife and a husband who live in harmony.

SIRACH 25:1

Grandchildren are the crown of the aged,
> and the glory of children is their parents.

PROVERBS 17:6

Sons are indeed a heritage from the LORD,
the fruit of the womb a reward.

PSALM 127:3–4

*Children, obey your parents in the Lord, for this is
right. "Honor your father and mother"—this is the
first commandment with a promise: "so that it may be
well with you and you may live long on the earth."
And fathers, do not provoke your children to anger,
but bring them up in the discipline and instruction of
the Lord.*

EPHESIANS 6:1–4

The father of the righteous will greatly rejoice;
> he who begets a wise son will be glad in him.

Let your father and mother be glad,
> let her who bore you rejoice.

PROVERBS 23:24–25

Family

Tell the older men to be temperate, serious, prudent, and sound in faith, in love, and in endurance. Likewise, tell the older women to be reverent in behavior, not to be slanderers or slaves to drink; they are to teach what is good, so that they may encourage the young women to love their husbands, to love their children, to be self-controlled, chaste, good managers of the household, kind, being submissive to their husbands so that the word of God may not be discredited.

TITUS 2:2–5

Those who honor their father will have joy in their own children,
>   and when they pray they will be heard.
Those who respect their father will have long life,
>   and those who honor their mother obey the Lord;
>   they will serve their parents as their masters.

SIRACH 3:5–7

Honor your mother and do not abandon her all the days of her life. Do whatever pleases her, and do not grieve her in anything.

TOBIT 4:3

Train children in the right way,
>   and when old, they will not stray.

PROVERBS 22:6

Family

A capable wife who can find?
  She is far more precious than jewels.
The heart of her husband trusts in her,
  and he will have no lack of gain. ...
Her children rise up and call her happy;
  her husband too, and he praises her.

PROVERBS 31:10–11,28–29

Choose this day whom you will serve ... but as for me and my household, we will serve the LORD.

JOSHUA 24:15

When a woman is in labor, she has pain, because her hour has come. But when her child is born, she no longer remembers the anguish because of the joy of having brought a human being into the world.

JOHN 16:21

I have no greater joy than this, to hear that my children are walking in the truth.

3 JOHN 4

In the fear of the LORD one has strong confidence,
  and one's children will have a refuge.

PROVERBS 14:26

It is all a prayer, that laundry. Not a chore—a task—an automated, get-it-out-of-the-way thing, but an opportunity to appreciate each member of the family. Doing the laundry, I have discovered, is a way to think about the gift of each person in my family. The sheets blowing on the line bring to mind the many moments of togetherness and intimacy shared in our marriage. As I iron the shirts of my husband, I remember his wonderful calming presence in my life. I smooth and fold the jeans of my son, thinking how this artist-child brings new, creative ways of thinking into my world. Large stacks of towels are simple reminders of the way my other son's presence is the gift of still and peaceful waters. Folding the underwear and sorting the socks, I remember my oldest daughter. Her depth and spiritual vision have shed light in my own inner life. The youngest child's zest for life comes to mind as my iron traces the fabric of colorful prints. Laundry is a way for me to give thanks for the gifts of my family.

Carol Gura

Forgiveness

You are a God ready to forgive, gracious and merciful,
slow to anger and abounding in steadfast love.

NEHEMIAH 9:17

Who is a God like you, pardoning iniquity
    and passing over the transgression
    of the remnant of your possession?
He does not retain his anger forever,
    because he delights in showing clemency.

MICAH 7:18

I am the LORD, your Holy One,
    the Creator of Israel, your King. ...
I, I am He
    who blots out your transgressions for my own sake,
    and I will not remember your sins.

ISAIAH 43:15, 25

Praise is due to you,
    O God, in Zion;
and to you shall vows be performed,
    O you who answer prayer!
To you all flesh shall come.
When deeds of iniquity overwhelm us,
    you forgive our transgressions.

PSALM 65:1–3

Forgiveness

God has rescued us from the power of darkness and transferred us into the kingdom of his beloved Son, in whom we have redemption, the forgiveness of sins.

COLOSSIANS 1:13–14

Whenever you stand praying, forgive, if you have anything against anyone; so that your Father in heaven may also forgive you your trespasses.

MARK 11:25

Thus says the LORD who made the earth, the LORD who formed it to establish it—the LORD is his name: ... I will cleanse them from all the guilt of their sin against me, and I will forgive all the guilt of their sin and rebellion against me.

JEREMIAH 33:2, 8

If we confess our sins, he who is faithful and just will forgive us our sins and cleanse us from all unrighteousness.

1 JOHN 1:9

Jesus said, "Father, hallowed be your name.
Your kingdom come.
Give us each day our daily bread,
And forgive us our sins,
    for we ourselves forgive everyone indebted to us.
And do not bring us to the time of trial."

LUKE 11:2-4

Forgiveness

*I forgive you all that you have done, says the
Lord GOD.*

EZEKIEL 16:63

*When you were dead in trespasses and the uncircumcision of your flesh, God made you alive together with
him, when he forgave us all our trespasses, erasing the
record that stood against us with its legal demands.
He set this aside, nailing it to the cross.*

COLOSSIANS 2:13–14

*In Christ we have redemption through his blood, the
forgiveness of our trespasses, according to the riches of
his grace that he lavished on us.*

EPHESIANS 1:7–8

The LORD is slow to anger,
and abounding in steadfast love,
forgiving iniquity and transgression,
but by no means clearing the guilty,

NUMBERS 14:18

The Lord is compassionate and merciful;
    he forgives sins and saves in time of distress.

SIRACH 2:11

Forgiveness

Do not judge, and you will not be judged; do not condemn, and you will not be condemned. Forgive, and you will be forgiven.

LUKE 6:37

Jesus said, "The one who believes and is baptized will be saved."

MARK 16:16

Let the wicked forsake their way
and the unrighteous their thoughts;
Let them return to the LORD, that he may have mercy on them
and to our God, for he will abundantly pardon.

ISAIAH 55:7

Bear with one another and if anyone has a complaint against another, forgive each other; just as the Lord has forgiven you, so you also must forgive.

COLOSSIANS 3:13

If you, O LORD, should mark iniquities,
Lord, who could stand?
But there is forgiveness with you,
so that you may be revered.

PSALM 130:3–4

Forgiveness

If anyone does sin, we have an advocate with the Father, Jesus Christ the righteous; and he is the atoning sacrifice for our sins, and not for ours only but also for the sins of the whole world.

1 John 2:1–2

Jesus said, "If you forgive others their trespasses, your heavenly Father will also forgive you."

Matthew 6:14

O Lord, hear; O Lord, forgive; O Lord, listen and act and do not delay!

Daniel 9:19

Peter came and said to him, "Lord, if another member of the church sins against me, how often should I forgive? As many as seven times?" Jesus said to him, "Not seven times, but, I tell you, seventy-seven times."

Matthew 18:21–22

They shall all know me, from the least of them to the greatest, says the LORD; for I will forgive their iniquity, and remember their sin no more.

Jeremiah 31:34

I often ask why people don't go to confession today more than they do. It can't be that we're sinning less. Can we have lost our appreciation for the sacrament of reconciliation because we no longer realize how terrible sin is? Do we no longer realize that all we have to do to claim the benefits of his suffering is to confess our sins and rely on his mercy?

When we go to confession, we realize that we fell, but Jesus forgives us. That's the beauty of our good and compassionate God.

It is true that Peter denied the Lord, but when the Lord looked at him, he repented and wept bitterly for his sin. (See "Well, I sinned and denied my master, but he has forgiven me." Judas couldn't forgive himself and couldn't accept God's forgiveness.

We must not allow guilt to beat us to the ground. It must not lead us into discouragement or depression. We have to keep humbling our-selves and saying, "Jesus, I did it again; please forgive me" and then get up and keep going.

Briege McKenna, O.S.C.

Friendship

A friend loves at all times,
and kinsfolk are born to share adversity.

PROVERBS 17:17

Faithful friends are a sturdy shelter;
whoever finds one has found a treasure.
Faithful friends are beyond price;
no amount can balance their worth.
Faithful friends are life-saving medicine;
and those who fear the Lord will find them.

SIRACH 6:14–16

Those who withhold kindness from a friend
forsake the fear of the Almighty.

JOB 6:14

Jesus said, "I do not call you servants any longer,
because the servant does not know what the master is
doing; but I have called you friends, because I have
made known to you everything that I have heard from
my Father."

JOHN 15:15

Love one another with mutual affection; outdo one
another in showing honor.

ROMANS 12:10

Friendship

I appeal to you, brothers and sisters, by the name of our Lord Jesus Christ, that all of you be in agreement and that there be no divisions among you, but that you be united in the same mind and the same purpose.

1 CORINTHIANS 1:10

Do not abandon old friends,
    for new ones cannot equal them.
A new friend is like new wine;
    when it has aged, you can drink it with pleasure.

SIRACH 9:10

The LORD used to speak to Moses face to face, as one speaks to a friend.

EXODUS 33:11

One who forgives an affront fosters friendship,
    but one who dwells on disputes will alienate a friend.

PROVERBS 17:9

Two are better than one, because they have a good reward for their toil. For if they fall, one will lift up the other; but woe to one who is alone and falls and does not have another to help.

ECCLESIASTES 4:9–10

Friendship

Some friends play at friendship
  but a true friend sticks closer than one's nearest kin.

PROVERBS 18:24

Wine and music gladden the heart,
  but the love of friends is better than either.

SIRACH 40:20

No one has greater love than this, to lay down one's life for one's friends.

JOHN 15:13

Do not exchange a friend for money, or a real brother for the gold of Ophir.

SIRACH 7:18

Love does no wrong to a neighbor; therefore, love is the fulfilling of the law.

ROMANS 13:10

Be quick to hear,
  but deliberate in answering
If you know what to say, answer your neighbor;
  but if not, put your hand over your mouth.

SIRACH 5:11–12

Those who love a pure heart and are gracious in speech
  will have the king as a friend.

PROVERBS 22:11

Sometimes I call a friend when my spirit or body needs support: a child is struggling, bronchitis strikes, or a relationship is strained. And friends come. They sit at the end of my bed or a telephone line and listen.

Friends bring wisdom, memories, and more questions. They hug us and cry at our predicaments.

Friends are responsible for each other. My friend Eileen can always be counted on to deliver her steaming pot of homemade chicken soup, fragrant with tomato, rice, potato, and onion. The food deliveries go both ways. Each one of us has gifts to offer as well as needs to be filled.

Anyone who is a friend, anyone who has a friend, knows that the relationship intensifies life's experiences and emotions. Friendship is a blessing. It is a gift. At a time when schedules and technologies can work against establishing and maintaining such relationships, friendships are worth the effort they require.

Saint Thomas Aquinas said that nothing on earth is more prized than true friendship. Jesus chose to be part of a web of friends while he walked the earth and shared our human existence. He continues to desire true friendship with each one of us. Our own friends are a reflection of that desire.

Mary Van Balen Holt

Fruit of the Spirit

The fruit of the Spirit is love, joy, peace, patience, kindness, generosity, faithfulness, gentleness, and self-control. There is no law against such things. And those who belong to Christ Jesus have crucified the flesh with its passions and desires. If we live by the Spirit let us also be guided by the Spirit.

GALATIANS 5:22–25

The sign of a happy heart is a cheerful face.

SIRACH 13:26

Jesus said, "The seed is the word of God. ... But as for that [seed] in the good soil, these are the ones who, when they hear the word, hold it fast in an honest and good heart, and bear fruit with patient endurance."

LUKE 8:11,15

The kingdom of God is not food and drink but righteousness and peace and joy in the Holy Spirit.

ROMANS 14:17

Do not be grieved for the joy of the LORD is your strength.

NEHEMIAH 8:10

Set your minds on things that are above, not on things that are on earth, for you have died, and your life is hidden with Christ in God.

COLOSSIANS 3:2

Fruit of the Spirit

We have gifts that differ according to the grace given to us: prophecy, in proportion to faith; ministry, in ministering; the teacher, in teaching; the exhorter, in exhortation; the giver, in generosity; the leader, in diligence; the compassionate, in cheerfulness.

ROMANS 12:6–8

Do your best to present yourself to God as one approved by him, a worker who has no need to be ashamed, rightly explaining the word of truth.

2 TIMOTHY 2:15

You must make every effort to support your faith with goodness and goodness with knowledge, and knowledge with self-control, and self-control with endurance, and endurance with godliness, and godliness with mutual affection, and mutual affection with love. For if these things are yours and are increasing among you, they keep you from being ineffective and unfruitful in the knowledge of our Lord Jesus Christ.

2 PETER 1:5–8

Jesus said, "Abide in me as I abide in you. Just as the branch cannot bear fruit by itself unless it abides in the vine, neither can you unless you abide in me."

JOHN 15:4

*F*ruit of the Spirit

You were taught to put away your former way of life, your old self, corrupt and deluded by its lusts, and to be renewed in the spirit of your minds, and to clothe yourselves with the new self, created according to the likeness of God in true righteousness and holiness.

EPHESIANS 4:22–24

This is my prayer, that your love may overflow more and more with knowledge and full insight to help you to determine what is best, so that in the day of Christ you may be pure and blameless, having produced the harvest of righteousness that comes through Jesus Christ for the glory and praise of God.

PHILIPPIANS 1:9–11

Rejoice in hope, be patient in suffering, persevere in prayer.

ROMANS 12:12

As God's chosen ones, holy and beloved, clothe yourselves with compassion, kindness, humility, meekness, and patience.

COLOSSIANS 3:12

*A*pple picking … It makes me think about the fruit of the Spirit. Bearing this kind of fruit doesn't require a talent that others admire. All it requires is yielding to the Holy Spirit and allowing the fruit of holiness to ripen.

The fruit of the Spirit is not primarily for our benefit, just as a tree doesn't bear fruit to hang there until it drops off and rots. The seeds of our fruit can over time bring forth more fruit. My joy can bring forth joy in another. My peace in a situation can help others be peaceful. My act of kindness or generosity can bear fruit in another—even if it may not mature in them for years. Bearing the fruit of the Spirit can bring exponential growth of goodness— and even holiness—to the world.

We are called to be Johnny Appleseeds of the soul, scattering seeds of holiness in our very beings, in our actions, in our words. As the saying goes, "Anyone can count the seeds in an apple, but only God can count the apples in a seed."

Wendy Leifield

God's Love

You love all things that exist,
    and detest none of the things that you have made,
    for you would not have made anything if you had
    hated it. ...
You spare all things, for they are yours, O Lord, you
who love the living.
For your immortal spirit is in all things.

THE WISDOM OF SOLOMON 11:24,26; 12:1

*Whoever does not love does not know God, for God is
love. God's love was revealed among us in this way:
God sent his only Son into the world so that we might
live through him. In this is love, not that we loved
God but that he loved us and sent his Son to be the
atoning sacrifice for our sins.*

1 JOHN 4:8–10

Let your steadfast love come to me, O LORD,
    your salvation according to your promise.
Then I shall have an answer for those who taunt me,
    for I trust in your word.

PSALM 119:41–42

I will sing of your might;
    I will sing aloud of your steadfast love in the
    morning.
For you have been a fortress for me
    and a refuge in the day of my distress.

PSALM 59:16

God's Love

Who will separate us from the love of Christ? Will hardship, or distress, or persecution, or famine, or nakedness, or peril, or sword? ... No, in all these things we are more than conquerors through him who loved us.

ROMANS 8:35,37

How precious is your steadfast love, O God!
> All people may take refuge in the shadow of
> your wings.

PSALM 36:7

I am convinced that neither death, nor life, nor angels, nor rulers, nor things present, nor things to come, nor powers, nor height, nor depth, nor anything else in all creation, will be able to separate us from the love of God in Christ Jesus our Lord.

ROMANS 8:38–39

Blessed be the LORD,
> for he has wondrously shown his steadfast love to me.

PSALM 31:21

Beloved, since God loved us so much, we also ought to love one another. No one has ever seen God; if we love one another, God lives in us, and his love is perfected in us.

1 JOHN 4:11–12

God's Love

Keep yourselves in the love of God; look forward to the mercy of our Lord Jesus Christ that leads to eternal life.

JUDE 21

Praise the LORD!
O give thanks to the LORD, for he is good;
    for his steadfast love endures forever.

PSALM 106:1

God's love has been poured into our hearts through the Holy Spirit that has been given to us. ... But God proves his love for us in that while we still were sinners Christ died for us.

ROMANS 5:5,8

God so loved the world that he gave his only Son, so that everyone who believes in him may not perish but may have eternal life.

JOHN 3:16

Jesus said, "For the Father himself loves you, because you have loved me and have believed that I came from God."

JOHN 16:27

*H*e showed me a little thing, the size of a hazelnut, in the palm of my hand, and it was a round as a ball. I looked at it with my mind's eye and I thought, "What can this be?" An answer came, "It is all that is made." I marveled that it could last, for I thought it might have crumbled to nothing, it was so small. And the answer came into my mind, "It lasts and ever shall because God loves it." And all things have being through the love of God.

In this little thing I saw three truths. The first is that God made it. The second is that God loves it. The third is that God looks after it.

What is he indeed that is maker and lover and keeper? I cannot find words to tell. For until I am one with him, I can never have true rest nor peace. I can never know it until I am held so close to him that there is nothing in between.

Julian of Norwich

God's Presence

Draw near to God and he will draw near to you.

JAMES 4:8

No one shall be able to stand against you all the days of your life. As I was with Moses, so I will be with you; I will not fail you or forsake you.

JOSHUA 1:5

God is not far from each one of us.

ACTS 17:27

Listen! I am standing at the door, knocking; if you hear my voice and open the door, I will come in to you and eat with you, and you with me.

REVELATION 3:20

The LORD, your God, is in your midst,
a warrior who gives victory;
he will rejoice over you with gladness,
he will renew you in his love;
he will exult over you with loud singing
as on a day of festival.

ZEPHANIAH 3:17–18

Know that I am with you and will keep you wherever you go, and will bring you back to this land; for I will not leave you until I have done what I have promised you.

GENESIS 28:15

God's Presence

Be strong and bold; have no fear or dread of them,
because it is the LORD your God who goes with you;
he will not fail you or forsake you.

DEUTERONOMY 31:6

Where can I go from your spirit?
Or where can I flee from you presence?
If I ascend to heaven, you are there;
    if I make my bed in Sheol, you are there.
If I take the wings of the morning
    and settle at the farthest limits of the sea,
even there your hand shall lead me,
    and your right hand shall hold me fast.

PSALM 139:7–10

You did not choose me but I chose you. And I
appointed you to go and bear fruit, fruit that will last,
so that the Father will give you whatever you ask him
in my name.

JOHN 15:16

The eyes of the LORD are on the righteous,
    and his ears are open to their cry. ...
When the righteous cry for help, the LORD hears,
    and rescues them from all their troubles.
The LORD is near to the brokenhearted,
    and saves the crushed in spirit.

PSALM 34:15,17–18

God's Presence

You will seek the LORD your God, and you will find him
if you search after him with all your heart and soul.

DEUTERONOMY 4:29

See, I have inscribed you on the palms of my hands.

ISAIAH 49:16

The LORD is my shepherd, I shall not want.
     He makes me lie down in green pastures;
he leads me beside still waters;
     he restores my soul.
He leads me in right paths
     for his name's sake.
Even though I walk through the darkest valley,
     I fear no evil;
for you are with me;
     your rod and your staff—
     they comfort me.
You prepare a table before me
     in the presence of my enemies,
you anoint my head with oil;
     my cup overflows
Surely goodness and mercy shall follow me
     all the days of my life
and I shall dwell in the house of the LORD
     my whole life long.

PSALM 23

$\mathcal{H}$old the mind in all simplicity and directness, without act or effort, in that simple gaze upon God and contemplation of God, in total surrender to his will; without a wish to see, or feel, or carry out any work, but merely content to remain in his presence—relaxed, at peace, confident, patient, never inspecting self to see how things are going, nor what one is doing, feeling or enduring. No, you must not inquire what your soul is doing, has done, or will do, nor what may happen to it in any future event or contingency. From this position you must not budge because this sole and single gaze upon God embraces all our duty, especially in a state of suffering. Hold fast to this simple state, and at the instant that you notice your mind drifting away from it, draw yourself back gently, without strain, or looking about, or self-direction, concerning anything whatever. One thing alone is necessary: It is to have God.

In short, then, no matter what is going on, we must hold both our attention and our love on God, not wasting our time in studying what is happening to ourselves, nor what is its cause. Our Lord asks this of us.

Saint Jeanne De Chantal

God's Will

It is God who is at work in you, enabling you both to will and to work for his good pleasure.

PHILIPPIANS 2:13

I cry to God Most High,
    to God who fulfills his purpose for me.

PSALM 57:2

Give thanks in all circumstances; for this is the will of God in Christ Jesus for you.

1 THESSALONIANS 5:18

I trust in you, O LORD;
    I say, "You are my God."
My times are in your hand;
        deliver me from the hand of my enemies and
        persecutors.

PSALM 31:14–15

Do not be conformed to this world, but be transformed by the renewing of your minds, so that you may discern what is the will of God—what is good and acceptable and perfect.

ROMANS 12:2

I delight to do your will, O my God;
    your law is within my heart.

PSALM 40:8

God's Will

This is the boldness we have in him, that if we ask anything according to his will, he hears us. And if we know that he hears us in whatever we ask, we know that we have obtained the requests made of him.

1 JOHN 5:14–15

Jesus said, "Whoever does the will of my Father in heaven is my brother and sister and mother."

MATTHEW 12:50

Commit your work to the LORD,
    and your plans will be established.

PROVERBS 16:3

Teach me to do your will,
    for you are my God.
Let your good spirit lead me
    on a level path.

PSALM 143:10

May the God of peace, who brought back from the dead our Lord Jesus, the great shepherd of the sheep, by the blood of the eternal covenant, make you complete in everything good so that you may do his will, working among us that which is pleasing in his sight, through Jesus Christ, to whom be the glory forever and ever. Amen.

HEBREWS 13:20–21

God's Will

Surely I know the plans I have for you, says the LORD, plans for your welfare and not for harm, to give you a future with hope.

JEREMIAH 29:11

The world and its desire are passing away, but those who do the will of God live forever.

1 JOHN 2:17

Everything that the Father gives me will come to me, and anyone who comes to me I will never drive away; for I have come down from heaven, not to do my own will, but the will of him who sent me. And this is the will of him who sent me, that I should lose nothing of all that he has given me, but raise it up on the last day. This is indeed the will of my Father, that all who see the Son and believe in him may have eternal life; and I will raise them up on the last day.

JOHN 6:37–40

God, who searches the heart knows what is the mind of the Spirit, because the Spirit intercedes for the saints according to the will of God. We know that all things work together for good for those who love God, who are called according to his purpose.

ROMANS 8:27–28

We are to do God's will in the time given to us: Now, later, tomorrow—carrying out God's will in the present moment, then in the moment that follows, until we reach the final moment, on which our eternity will depend.

We are not to dwell on the past or dream about the future. The past should be left to God's mercy, since it is no longer ours; and the future will only be fully lived when it becomes the present.

Only the present is in our hands. So that if God is to reign in our lives, we must concentrate our whole mind, heart and strength on the accomplishment of his will here and now.

Just as a traveler in a train would not think of moving forward through the cars so as to get to his destination sooner, but remains seated and lets the train carry him along, so our souls, to get to God, should fulfill, wholeheartedly, his will in the present movement, since time moves forward on its own.

Chiara Lubich

Grace

By grace you have been saved through faith, and this is not your own doing; it is the gift of God—not the result of works, so that no one may boast.

EPHESIANS 2:8–9

All have sinned and fall short of the glory of God; they are now justified by his grace as a gift, through the redemption that is in Christ Jesus, whom God put forward as a sacrifice of atonement by his blood effective through faith.

ROMANS 3:23–25

Those who trust in God will understand truth,
    and the faithful will abide with him in love,
because grace and mercy are upon his holy ones,
    and he watches over his elect.

THE WISDOM OF SOLOMON 3:9

When the goodness and loving kindness of God our Savior appeared, he saved us, not because of any works of righteousness that we had done, but according to his mercy, through the water of rebirth and renewal by the Holy Spirit. This Spirit he poured out on us richly through Jesus Christ our Savior, so that, having been justified by his grace, we might become heirs according to the hope of eternal life.

TITUS 3:4–7

······································

Grace

*Christ also suffered for sins once for all, the righteous
for the unrighteous, in order to bring you to God.*

1 PETER 3:18

Happy are those whose transgression is forgiven,
    whose sin is covered.
Happy are those to whom the LORD imputes no iniquity,
    and in whose spirit there is no deceit.

PSALM 32:1–2

*The grace of God has appeared, bringing salvation
to all, training us to renounce impiety and worldly
passions, and in the present age to live lives that are
self-controlled, upright and godly, while we wait for
the blessed hope and the manifestation of the glory of
our great God and Savior, Jesus Christ.*

TITUS 2:11–13

*Since we are justified by faith, we have peace with
God through our Lord Jesus Christ, through whom
we have obtained access to this grace in which we
stand; and we boast in our hope of sharing the glory
of God.*

ROMANS 5:1–2

Therefore the LORD waits to be gracious to you;
    therefore he will rise up to show mercy to you.
For the LORD is a God of justice;
    blessed are all those who wait for him.

ISAIAH 30:18

Grace

God raised us up with him and seated us with him in the heavenly places in Christ Jesus, so that in the ages to come he might show the immeasurable riches of his grace in kindness toward us in Christ Jesus.

EPHESIANS 2:6–7

We believe that we will be saved through the grace of the Lord Jesus, just as they will.

ACTS 15:11

The LORD your God is gracious and merciful, and will not turn away his face from you, if you return to him.

2 CHRONICLES 30:9

The free gift is not like the trespass. For if the many died through the one man's trespass, much more surely have the grace of God and the free gift in the grace of the one man, Jesus Christ, abounded for the many.

ROMANS 5:15

From his fullness we have all received, grace upon grace. The law indeed was given through Moses; grace and truth came through Jesus Christ.

JOHN 1:16–17

This is our boast, the testimony of our conscience: we have behaved in the world with frankness and godly sincerity, not by earthly wisdom but by the grace of God.

2 CORINTHIANS 1:12

Grace

O LORD, be gracious to us; we wait for you.
> Be our arm every morning,
> our salvation in the time of trouble.

ISAIAH 33:2

The hand of our God is gracious to all who seek him,
but his power and his wrath are against all who
forsake him.

EZRA 8:22

The Word became flesh and lived among us, and we
have seen his glory, the glory as of a father's only son,
full of grace and truth.

JOHN 1:14

Let us therefore approach the throne of grace with
boldness, so that we may receive mercy and find grace
to help in time of need.

HEBREWS 4:16

If anyone is in Christ, there is a new creation:
everything old has passed away; see, everything has
become new!

2 CORINTHIANS 5:17

Grace

There is therefore now no condemnation for those who are in Christ Jesus. For the law of the Spirit of life in Christ Jesus has set you free from the law of sin and of death.

ROMANS 8:1–2

Gracious is the LORD, and righteous;
  our God is merciful.
The LORD protects the simple;
  when I was brought low, he saved me.

PSALM 116:5–6

The wages of sin is death, but the free gift of God is eternal life in Christ Jesus our Lord.

ROMANS 6:23

May our Lord Jesus Christ himself and God our Father, who loved us and through grace gave us eternal comfort and good hope, comfort your hearts and strengthen them in every good work and word.

2 THESSALONIANS 2:16–17

The grace of the Lord Jesus be with all the saints. Amen.

REVELATION 22:21

New England on a cool, crisp fall day; the Midwest during summer, where farmland stretches way beyond what I can see; the West Coast, or way down south or on one of the islands where I can hear all sorts of beautiful sounds from a vast array of birds—these scenes are endless in my mind. All of them produce the same experience for me—a sense of newness, freshness, peacefulness, stillness, calm—another day, another start. Untouched, clean, ready to experience all that life has to offer once again.

I am constantly reminded of the faithfulness of God and that his mercies are new every morning. What I was yesterday, what I felt yesterday, what I did yesterday is covered by his grace. He remembers it no more. He throws it as far as the east is from the west— as I turn, as I repent, as I offer him my sins, my failures, and even the consequences of my choices. There is so much beauty to the morning, and there is so much beauty in a heart filled with the certainty that the Lord has once again come to fill, restore, and heal.

His steadfast love never ceases. His mercies never end.

Kathy Troccoli

Gratitude

Be generous when you worship the Lord,
> and do not stint the first fruits of your hands.
With every gift show a cheerful face,
> and dedicate your tithe with gladness.
Give to the Most High as he has given to you,
> and as generously as you can afford.
For the Lord is the one who repays,
> and he will repay you sevenfold.

SIRACH 35:10–13

Let them thank the LORD for his steadfast love,
> for his wonderful works to humankind.
And let them offer thanksgiving sacrifices,
> and tell of his deeds with songs of joy.

PSALM 107:21–22

Thanks be to God, who gives us the victory through our Lord Jesus Christ.

1 CORINTHIANS 15:57

As you therefore have received Christ Jesus the Lord, continue to live your lives in him, rooted and built up in him and established in the faith, just as you were taught, abounding in thanksgiving.

COLOSSIANS 2:6–7

Gratitude

Praise the LORD!
How good it is to sing praises to our God;
for he is gracious, and a song of praise is fitting. ...
Sing to the LORD with thanksgiving;
make melody to our God on the lyre.

PSALM 147:1,7

O give thanks to the LORD, call on his name,
make known his deeds among the peoples.
Sing to him, sing praises to him,
tell of all his wonderful works.

1 CHRONICLES 16:8–9

Be filled with the Spirit, as you sing psalms and
hymns and spiritual songs among yourselves, singing
and making melody to the Lord in your hearts, giving
thanks to God the Father at all times and for every-
thing in the name of our Lord Jesus Christ.

EPHESIANS 5:18–20

In everything, O Lord, you have exalted and glorified
your people,
and you have not neglected to help them at all times
and in all places.

THE WISDOM OF SOLOMON 19:22

Gratitude

O come, let us sing to the LORD;
> let us make a joyful noise to the rock of our
> salvation!
Let us come into his presence with thanksgiving;
> let us make a joyful noise to him with songs of
> praise!

PSALM 95:1–2

O give thanks to the LORD, for he is good;
> for his steadfast love endures forever.

PSALM 107:1

*Let the peace of Christ rule in your hearts, to which
indeed you were called in the one body. And be
thankful. ... And whatever you do, in word or deed,
do everything in the name of the Lord Jesus, giving
thanks to God the Father through him.*

COLOSSIANS 3:15,17

Praise the LORD!
I will give thanks to the LORD with my whole heart,
> in the company of the upright, in the congregation.
Great are the works of the LORD,
> studied by all who delight in them.

PSALM 111:1-2

*Thanks be to God, who in Christ always leads us in
triumphal procession, and through us spreads in every
place the fragrance that comes from knowing him.*

2 CORINTHIANS 2:14

There are so many ways of praying, so many ways of addressing God: in repentance, in petition, in intercession. But in the end, we were made to praise our Creator. Gratitude puts everything into a different perspective. It prevents me from taking anything for granted. It helps me to live my life awake, alert to those good gifts that I am given, in a state of mindfulness or awareness. Then, when I look at the world with eyes of wonder, I discover, rather to my chagrin, that it is often only too easy to drift and become neglectful, lazy, forgetful of gratefulness.

I enjoy that line of W. H. Auden, "Practice the scales of rejoicing," because of its suggestion that it really is hard work and needs discipline. I might rewrite those familiar words "pray without ceasing" so that they become "praise without ceasing," giving thanks to my Creator for all the good gifts in my life.

Esther De Waal

Holiness

Consecrate yourselves therefore, and be holy; for I am the LORD your God.

LEVITICUS 20:7

Who is like you, O LORD, among the gods?
    Who is like you, majestic in holiness,
    awesome in splendor, doing wonder?
You stretched out your right hand,
    the earth swallowed them.
In your steadfast love you led the people whom you redeemed;
    you guided them by your strength to your holy abode.

EXODUS 15:11–13

God's grace and mercy are with his elect,
    and… he watches over his holy ones.

THE WISDOM OF SOLOMON 4:15

God did not call us to impurity but in holiness.

1 THESSALONIANS 4:7

They will be made holy who observe holy things in holiness,
and those who have been taught them will find a defense.
Therefore set your desire on my words;
long for them, and you will be instructed.

THE WISDOM OF SOLOMON 6:10–11

Holiness

Pursue peace with everyone, and the holiness without which no one will see the Lord. See to it that no one fails to obtain the grace of God; that no root of bitterness springs up and causes trouble, and through it many become defiled.

HEBREWS 12:14–15

I am the LORD your God, sanctify yourselves therefore, and be holy, for I am holy.

LEVITICUS 11:44

May our God and Father himself and our Lord Jesus direct our way to you. ... And may he so strengthen your hearts in holiness that you may be blameless before our God and Father at the coming of our Lord Jesus with all his saints.

1 THESSALONIANS 3:11,13

As he who called you is holy, be holy yourselves in all your conduct; for it is written, "You shall be holy, for I am holy."

1 PETER 1:15–16

I will display my greatness and my holiness and make myself known in the eyes of many nations. Then they shall know that I am the LORD.

EZEKIEL 38:23

Holiness

Since we have these promises, beloved, let us cleanse ourselves from every defilement of body and of spirit, making holiness perfect in the fear of God.

2 CORINTHIANS 7:1

God's divine power has given us everything needed for life and godliness, through the knowledge of him who called us by his own glory and goodness.

2 PETER 1:3

Whatever is true, whatever is honorable, whatever is just, whatever is pure, whatever is pleasing, whatever is commendable, if there is any excellence and if there is anything worthy of praise, think about these things.

PHILIPPIANS 4:8

They disciplined us for a short time as seemed best to them, but he disciplines us for our good, in order that we may share his holiness.

HEBREWS 12:10

You are a chosen race, a royal priesthood, a holy nation, God's own people, in order that you may proclaim the mighty acts of him who called you out of darkness into his marvelous light.

1 PETER 2:9

*O*ne night, I woke up with a start. I looked up at the ceiling and there was a picture of a beautiful garden. The garden had many flowers and among these flowers were little weeds.

The Lord said to me, "Briege, this is your soul." The flowers represented the virtues I was trying to cultivate in my efforts to become holy. As I walked around the garden admiring the flowers, I was looking at the weeds saying, "Oh, they're just small and they won't do a bit of harm."

Then the Lord said, "Those weeds represent sin. You are comparing yourself with all the evil in the world. You are not called to compare yourself with the world. You are called to compare yourself with me. I am your model. Not the world. You must never accept sin. If you let me, I'll eradicate those weeds for you. Then the flowers will have a brighter color and there will be greater growth in your garden."

The Lord showed me two things through this image. First, I cannot save myself. I cannot make my garden beautiful on my own; I cannot become holy on my own. I must acknowledge that I am a sinner. If I don't, I am self-righteous and proud. Second, I learned the value of repentance and the beauty of confession. Confession is coming to the Jesus who loves me.

Briege McKenna, O.S.C.

Hope

The spirit of those who fear the Lord will live,
    for their hope is in him who saves them.
Those who fear the Lord will not be timid,
    or play the coward, for he is their hope.

SIRACH 34:14–15

*We have this hope, a sure and steadfast anchor of the
soul, a hope that enters the inner shrine behind the
curtain, where Jesus, a forerunner on our behalf, has
entered, having become a high priest forever.*

HEBREWS 6:19–20

*Through Christ you have come to trust in God, who
raised him from the dead and gave him glory, so that
your faith and hope are set on God.*

1 PETER 1:21

Truly the eye of the LORD is on those who fear him,
    on those who hope in his steadfast love.

PSALM 33:18

Our soul waits for the LORD;
    he is our help and shield.
Our heart is glad in him,
    because we trust in his holy name.
Let your steadfast love, O LORD,
    be upon us, even as we hope in you.

PSALM 33:20–22

Hope

Rejoice in hope, be patient in suffering, persevere in prayer.

ROMANS 12:12

Take courage, my children, cry to God,
    and he will deliver you from the power and hand
        of the enemy.
For I have put my hope in the Everlasting to save you,
    and joy has come to me from the Holy One,
because of the mercy that will soon come to you
    from your everlasting savior.

BARUCH 4:21–22

Why are you cast down, O my soul,
    and why are you disquieted within me?
Hope in God; for I shall again praise him,
    my help and my God.

PSALM 42:11

Blessed be the God and Father of our Lord Jesus Christ! By his great mercy he has given us a new birth into a living hope through the resurrection of Jesus Christ from the dead, and into an inheritance that is imperishable, undefiled, and unfading, kept in heaven for you, who are being protected by the power of God through faith for a salvation ready to be revealed in the last time.

1 PETER 1:3–5

*H*ope

God who rescued us from so deadly a peril will
continue to rescue us; on him we have set our hope
that he will rescue us again.

2 CORINTHIANS 1:10

Even youths will faint and be weary,
    and the young will fall exhausted;
but those who wait for the LORD shall renew their
    strength,
       they shall mount up with wings like eagles,
they shall run and not be weary,
    they shall walk and not faint.

ISAIAH 40:30–31

You, O Lord, are my hope,
my trust, O LORD, from my youth.

PSALM 71:5

"The LORD is my portion," says my soul,
    "therefore I will hope in him."

LAMENTATIONS 3:24

Know that wisdom is such to your soul;
    if you find it, you will find a future,
    and your hope will not be cut off.

PROVERBS 24:14

Hope

May the God of hope fill you with all joy and peace in believing, so that you may abound in hope by the power of the Holy Spirit.

ROMANS 15:13

Beloved, we are God's children now; what we will be has not yet been revealed. What we do know is this: when he is revealed, we will be like him, for we will see him as he is. And all who have this hope in him purify themselves, just as he is pure.

1 JOHN 3:2–3

I will hope continually,
    and will praise you yet more and more.
My mouth will tell of your righteous acts,
    of your deeds of salvation all day long,
       though their number is past my knowledge.

PSALM 71:14–15

Whatever was written in former days was written for our instruction, so that by steadfastness and by the encouragement of the scriptures we might have hope.

ROMANS 15:4

Hope deferred makes the heart sick,
    but a desire fulfilled is a tree of life.

PROVERBS 13:12

Hope

Happy are those whose help is the God of Jacob,
　　whose hope is in the LORD their God,
who made heaven and earth,
　　the sea, and all that is in them;
who keeps faith forever;
　　who executes justice for the oppressed;
　　who gives food to the hungry.

PSALM 146:5–7

In hope we were saved. Now hope that is seen is not
hope. For who hopes for what is seen? But if we hope
for what we do not see, we wait for it with patience.

ROMANS 8:24–25

O Israel, hope in the LORD!
　　For with the LORD there is steadfast love,
　　and with him is great power to redeem.
It is he who will redeem Israel
　　from all its iniquities.

PSALM 130:7–8

O Israel, hope in the LORD
　　from this time on and
　　forevermore.

PSALM 131:3

*T*ake time alone and in silence today to reflect on the gift of hope, which has been freely given to you at Baptism. Pray this prayer often during the day, asking God to rekindle and enlarge this gift of hope.

God, you are like a mother hen, gathering her chicks, watching over them with loving care. Help me to place my hope in your promise to care for and watch over me and those I love.

God, you are [like] the baker woman who knows the miraculous capacity of yeast to raise a whole loaf of bread. I hope in this same miraculous power of your Spirit to penetrate my whole being and fill me with an enthusiasm for life and love. I place my entire hope in your mysterious ways of kneading the yeast of your Spirit into my entire family, my faith community, and even this world.

God, you are the bridegroom who calls me like a lover and companion. Increase my hope that you delight in me, love me unconditionally and have made me for goodness.

God of Mary, Mother of Sorrows, Woman of Hope, even in the impossible, foster a deeper sense of hope in me. Amen.

Carol Gura

Humility

Seek the LORD, all you humble of the land,
    who do his commands;
seek righteousness, seek humility;
      perhaps you may be hidden
      on the day of the LORD'S wrath.

ZEPHANIAH 2:3

*If my people who are called by my name humble
themselves, pray, seek my face, and turn from their
wicked ways, then I will hear from heaven, and will
forgive their sin and heal their land.*

2 CHRONICLES 7:14

Do not boast about wearing fine clothes,
    and do not exalt yourself when you are honored;
for the works of the Lord are wonderful,
    and his works are concealed from humankind.

SIRACH 11:4

You deliver a humble people,
    but the haughty eyes you bring down.

PSALM 18:27

When pride comes, then comes disgrace;
    but wisdom is with the humble.

PROVERBS 11:2

Humility

Thus says the LORD:
Heaven is my throne
     and the earth is my footstool;
what is the house that you would build for me,
     and what is my resting place?
All these things my hand has made,
     and so all these things are mine, says the LORD.
But this is the one to whom I will look,
     to the humble and contrite in spirit,
     who trembles at my word.

ISAIAH 66:1–2

The man Moses was very humble, more so than
anyone else on the face of the earth.

NUMBERS 12:3

Clothe yourselves with humility in your dealings with
one another, for
     "God opposes the proud,
     but gives grace to the humble."
Humble yourselves therefore under the mighty hand
of God, so that he may exalt you in due time.

1 PETER 5:5–6

The LORD takes pleasure in his people;
     he adorns the humble with victory.

PSALM 149:4

*H*umility

*Do nothing from selfish ambition or conceit, but in
humility regard others as better than yourselves.*

PHILIPPIANS 2:3

The fear of the Lord is wisdom and discipline,
    fidelity and humility are his delight.

SIRACH 1:27

*Jesus said, "The greatest among you will be your
servant. All who exalt themselves will be humbled,
and all who humble themselves will be exalted."*

MATTHEW 23:11–12

He has told you, O mortal, what is good;
    and what does the LORD require of you
but to do justice, and to love kindness,
    and to walk humbly with your God?

MICAH 6:8

My child, perform your tasks with humility;
    then you will be loved by those whom God accepts.
The greater you are, the more you must humble yourself;
    so you will find favor in the sight of the Lord.
For great is the might of the Lord;
    but by the humble he is glorified.

SIRACH 3:17–20

*K*nowledge of the self puts us on our knees, and it is very necessary for love. For knowledge of God produces love, and knowledge of the self produces humility. Knowledge of the self is a very important thing in our lives. As Saint Augustine says, "Fill yourselves first, and then only will you be able to give to others."

Knowledge of the self is also a safeguard against pride, especially when you are tempted in life. The greatest mistake is to think you are too strong to fall into temptation. Put your finger in the fire and it will burn. So we have to go through the fire. The temptations are allowed by God. The only thing we have to do is to refuse to give in.

Mother Teresa of Calcutta

Identity

See what love the Father has given us, that we should be called children of God; and that is what we are.

1 JOHN 3:1

Do you not know that your body is a temple of the Holy Spirit within you, which you have from God, and that you are not your own? For you were bought with a price; therefore glorify God in your body.

1 CORINTHIANS 6:19–20

God said, "Let us make humankind in our image, according to our likeness; and let them have dominion over the fish of the sea, and over the birds of the air, and over the cattle, and over all the wild animals of the earth, and over every creeping thing that creeps upon the earth."

So God created humankind in his image,
in the image of God he created them;
male and female he created them.

GENESIS 1:26–27

In fulfillment of his own purpose he gave us birth by the word of truth, so that we would become a kind of first fruits of his creatures.

JAMES 1:18

If we live, we live to the Lord, and if we die, we die to the Lord; so then, whether we live or whether we die, we are the Lord's.

ROMANS 14:8

Identity

Because you are children, God has sent the Spirit of his Son into our hearts, crying, "Abba! Father!" So you are no longer a slave but a child, and if a child then also an heir, through God.

GALATIANS 4:6–7

When I look at your heavens, the work of your fingers,
   the moon and the stars that you have established;
what are human beings that you are mindful of them,
   mortals that you care for them?
Yet you have made them a little lower than God,
   and crowned them with glory and honor.

PSALM 8:3–5

You have been born anew, not of perishable but of imperishable seed, through the living and enduring word of God.

1 PETER 1:23

We are ambassadors for Christ, since God is making his appeal through us; we entreat you on behalf of Christ, be reconciled to God.

2 CORINTHIANS 5:20

Do not lie to one another, seeing that you have stripped off the old self with its practices and have clothed yourselves with the new self, which is being renewed in knowledge according to the image of its creator.

COLOSSIANS 3:9–10

Identity

When we cry, "Abba! Father!" it is that very Spirit bearing witness with our spirit that we are children of God, and if children then heirs, heirs of God and joint heirs with Christ—if, in fact, we suffer with him so that we may also be glorified with him.

ROMANS 8:16–17

Do you not know that you are God's temple and that God's Spirit dwells in you? If anyone destroys God's temple, God will destroy that person. For God's temple is holy, and you are that temple.

1 CORINTHIANS 3:16

Now that faith has come, we are no longer subject to a disciplinarian, for in Christ Jesus you are all children of God through faith. As many of you as were baptized into Christ have clothed yourselves with Christ. There is no longer Jew or Greek, there is no longer slave or free, there is no longer make and female; for all of you are one in Christ Jesus.

GALATIANS 3:25–29

When Christ who is your life is revealed, then you also will be revealed with him in glory.

COLOSSIANS 3:4

If anyone is in Christ, there is a new creation: everything old has passed away; see, everything has become new!

2 CORINTHIANS 5:17

Identity

'In him we live and move and have our being', as even some of your own poets have said, 'For we too are his offspring.'

ACTS 17:28

It was you who formed my inward parts;
   you knit me together in my mother's womb.
I praise you, for I am fearfully and wonderfully made.
   Wonderful are your works;
that I know very well.

PSALM 139:13–14

In Christ the whole fullness of deity dwells bodily, and you have come to fullness in him, who is the head of every ruler and authority.

COLOSSIANS 2:9–10

Jesus said, "Are not five sparrows sold for two pennies? Yet not one of them is forgotten in God's sight. But even the hairs of your head are all counted. Do not be afraid; you are of more value than many sparrows."

LUKE 12:6–7

Before I formed you in the womb I knew you,
and before you were born I consecrated you.

JEREMIAH 1:5

A person's attire and hearty laughter,
   and the way he walks, show what he is.

SIRACH 19:30

Identity

O come, let us worship and bow down,
>   let us kneel before the LORD, our Maker!
For he is our God,
>   and we are the people of his pasture,
>   and the sheep of his hand.

PSALM 95:6–7

>   My frame was not hidden from you,
when I was being made in secret,
>   intricately woven in the depths of the earth.
Your eyes beheld my unformed substance.
In your book were written
>   all the days that were formed for me,
>   when none of them as yet existed.

PSALM 139:15–18

Know that the LORD is God,
>   it is he that made us, and we are his;
>   we are his people, and the sheep of his pasture.

PSALM 100:3

*You are no longer strangers and aliens, but you are
citizens with the saints and also members of the
household of God, built upon the foundation of the
apostles and prophets, with Christ Jesus himself as
the cornerstone.*

EPHESIANS 2:19–20

*W*hen we first come to the Lord, we try to hide behind our pretenses, to be some other person that we think we are supposed to be. But the more we get to know him, the more we discover that he has created us to be ourselves. And we discover this little by little. Like patients at the first therapy session, we blurt out to the Lord everything we hate ourselves for, fully expecting to be able to shock him. The Lord retains his composure. His compassion is inexhaustible.

When we begin to experience that forgiveness personally, it no longer seems to matter that he offers it to the whole world, for each of us knows that the Lord is giving it "just" to him [or her]. In this encounter we become aware of the wonder of the individual. God has made me; I am unique, even with all my faults I am worthwhile; this kind of self-discovery is strengthening and restoring; loving the Lord makes it possible to love ourselves in ways that are constructive and healthy. We grow to know ourselves better in the light he pours into our lives; we come to see what it is that he loves in us, how pleasing we are to him.

Emilie Griffin

$\mathcal{L}$ove for Others

Jesus said, "I give you a new commandment, that you love one another. Just as I have loved you, you also should love one another. By this everyone will know that you are my disciples, if you have love for one another."

JOHN 13:34–35

Jesus said, "I say to you that listen, Love your enemies, do good to those who hate you, bless those who curse you, pray for those who abuse you."

LUKE 6:27–28

The fruit of the Spirit is love, joy, peace, patience, kindness, generosity, faithfulness, gentleness, and self-control. There is no law against such things.

GALATIANS 5:22

Love is patient, love is kind; love is not envious or boastful or arrogant or rude. It does not insist on its own way; it is not irritable or resentful; it does not rejoice in wrongdoing, but rejoices in the truth.

1 CORINTHIANS 13:4–6

You shall not take vengeance or bear a grudge against any of your people, but you shall love your neighbor as yourself: I am the LORD.

LEVITICUS 19:18

*L*ove for Others

*In Christ Jesus neither circumcision nor
uncircumcision counts for anything; the only thing
that counts is faith working through love.*

GALATIANS 5:6

*The alien who resides with you shall be to you as the
citizen among you; you shall love the alien as yourself,
for you were aliens in the land of Egypt: I am the
LORD your God.*

LEVITICUS 19:34

*Jesus said, "No one has greater love than this, to lay
down one's life for one's friends".*

JOHN 15:13

*Jonathan made a covenant with the house of David,
saying "May the LORD seek out the enemies of
David." Jonathan made David swear again by his
love for him; for he loved him as he loved his own life.*

1 SAMUEL 20:16–17

How very good and pleasant it is
    when kindred live together in unity!

PSALM 133:1

Hatred stirs up strife,
    but love covers all offenses.

PROVERBS 10:12

Love for Others

You do well if you really fulfill the royal law according to the scripture, "You shall love your neighbor as yourself."

JAMES 2:8

You were called to freedom, brothers and sisters; only do not use your freedom as an opportunity for self-indulgence, but through love become slaves to one another. For the whole law is summed up in a single commandment, "You shall love your neighbor as yourself."

GALATIANS 5:13–14

We know love by this, that he laid down his life for us —and we ought to lay down our lives for one another.

1 JOHN 3:16

As God's chosen ones, holy and beloved, clothe yourselves with compassion, kindness, humility, meekness, and patience. ... Above all, clothe yourselves with love which binds everything together in perfect harmony.

COLOSSIANS 3:12,14

You yourselves have been taught by God to love one another.

1 THESSALONIANS 4:9

Whoever loves a brother or sister lives in the light, and in such a person there is no cause for stumbling.

1 JOHN 2:10

Love for Others

Jesus said, "You have heard that it was said, 'You shall love your neighbor and hate your enemy.' But I say to you, Love your enemies and pray for those who persecute you, so that you may be children of your Father in heaven; for he makes his sun rise on the evil and on the good, and sends rain on the righteous and on the unrighteous."

MATTHEW 5:43–45

Above all, maintain constant love for one another, for love covers a multitude of sins. Be hospitable to one another without complaining. Like good stewards of the manifold grace of God, serve one another with whatever gift each of you has received.

1 PETER 4:8–10

The commandment we have from him is this: those who love God must love their brothers and sisters also.

1 JOHN 4:21

God did not give us a spirit of cowardice, but rather a spirit of power and of love and of self-discipline.

2 TIMOTHY 1:7

Whenever we have an opportunity, let us work for the good of all, and especially for those of the family of faith.

GALATIANS 6:10

Love for Others

Let mutual love continue. Do not neglect to show hospitality to strangers, for by doing that some have entertained angels without knowing it.

HEBREWS 13:1–2

Now that you have purified your souls by your obedience to the truth so that you have genuine mutual love, love one another deeply from the heart.

1 PETER 1:22

Beloved, let us love one another, because love is from God; everyone who loves is born of God and knows God. Whoever does not love does not know God, for God is love.

1 JOHN 4:7–8

Be imitators of God, as beloved children, and live in love, as Christ loved us and gave himself up for us, a fragrant offering and sacrifice to God.

EPHESIANS 5:1–2

We love because he first loved us.

1 JOHN 4:19

May the Lord make you increase and abound in love for one another and for all, just as we abound in love for you.

1 THESSALONIANS 3:12

Some time ago a man came to our house and said, "Mother, there is a Hindu family that has eight children. They have not eaten for a long time. Do something for them." So I took some rice and went. I gave the rice to the mother. She took it and divided it into two, and then she went out. When she came back, I asked her, "Where did you go?" She said, "They are hungry also."

Love, to be true, has to hurt, and this woman who was hungry—she knew that her neighbor was also hungry. That family happened to be a Mohammedan family. It was so touching, so real. This is where we are most unjust to our poor—we don't know them. We don't know how great they are, how lovable, how hungry for that understanding love. Today God loves the world through you and through me. Are we that love and that compassion? God proves that Christ loves us—that he has come to be his Father's compassion. Today God is loving the world through you and through me and through all those who are his love and compassion in the world.

Mother Teresa of Calcutta

ℳarriage

I found him whom my soul loves.
I held him, and would not let him go.

SONG OF SOLOMON 3:4

*Husbands should love their wives as they do their
own bodies. He who loves his wife loves himself. For
no one ever hates his own body, but he nourishes and
tenderly cares for it, just as Christ does for the church.*

EPHESIANS 5:28–29

*If anyone thinks that he is not behaving properly
toward his fiancée, if his passions are strong, and so it
has to be, let him marry as he wishes; it is no sin. Let
them marry.*

1 CORINTHIANS 7:36

Happy is the husband of a good wife;
    the number of his days will be doubled.
A loyal wife brings joy to her husband,
    and he will complete his years in peace.
A good wife is a great blessing;
    she will be granted among the blessings of the
    man who fears the Lord.
Whether rich or poor, his heart is content,
    and at all times his face is cheerful.

SIRACH 26:1–4

Let all that you do be done in love.

1 CORINTHIANS 16:14

$\mathcal{M}$arriage

Greet one another with a kiss of love.

1 PETER 5:14

Enjoy life with the wife whom you love.

ECCLESIASTES 9:9

*Each man should have his own wife and each woman
her own husband. The husband should give to his
wife her conjugal rights, and likewise the wife to her
husband. For the wife does not have authority over
her own body, but the husband does; likewise the
husband does not have authority over his own body,
but the wife does. Do not deprive one another except
perhaps by agreement for a set time, to devote yourselves to prayer, and then come together again, so
that Satan may not tempt you because of your lack of
self-control.*

1 CORINTHIANS 7:2–5

Set me as a seal upon your heart,
    as a seal upon your arm;
for love is strong as death, passion fierce as the grave.
Its flashes are flashes of fire, a raging flame.
Many waters cannot quench love,
    neither can floods drown it.
If one offered for love
    all the wealth of one's house,
    it would be utterly scorned.

SONG OF SOLOMON 8:6–7

$\mathcal{M}$arriage

Cattle and orchards make one prosperous;
>   but a blameless wife is accounted better than either.

SIRACH 40:19

You must understand this, my beloved, let everyone be quick to listen, slow to speak, slow to anger; for your anger does not produce God's righteousness.

JAMES 1:19

This is the message you have heard form the beginning, that we should love one another.

1 JOHN 3:11

Let marriage be held in honor by all, and let the marriage bed be kept undefiled; for God will judge fornicators and adulterers.

HEBREWS 13:4

There is no fear in love, but perfect love casts out fear; for fear has to do with punishment, and whoever fears has not reached perfection in love.

1 JOHN 4:18

*I*n big ways and small, marriage always calls a man and a woman to self-giving love of each other and of their children. But when spouses base their marriage on Jesus Christ, their covenant becomes a sacrament with an even deeper call: They are to model Christ's redemptive love. They themselves become sacred signs of how Christ relates to the Church. Indeed, as Saint Paul muses, "This is a great mystery." (See Ephesians 5:28-32.)

Jesus is the church's bridegroom. The theme is developed in Scripture, though gradually, by prophets such as Hosea and in the Song of Solomon's lyrical description of married love. But no less amazing is the bridegroom's call to every Christian couple. In a symbolic but real way, every married couple—even Steve and Jane down the street—are to make visible the mystery of Christ's love for the church.

This is where sacramental grace comes in. Without the life and power of the Holy Spirit, husband and wife are helpless to fulfill their high calling. With it, though, they will find all they need—faith, perseverance, and deepening love for every challenge of married life.

Louise Perrotta

Mercy

Jesus said, "Blessed are the merciful, for they will receive mercy."

MATTHEW 5:7

Thus says the LORD of hosts: Render true judgments, show kindness and mercy to one another.

ZECHARIAH 7:9

I will sing to my God a new song:
O Lord, you are great and glorious,
    wonderful in strength, invincible. ...
For the mountains shall be shaken to their
foundations with the waters;
    before your glance the rocks shall melt like wax.
But to those who fear you
    you show mercy.

JUDITH 16:13,15

No one who conceals transgressions will prosper,
    but one who confesses and forsakes them will
      obtain mercy.

PROVERBS 28:13

Is there injustice on God's part? By no means! For he says to Moses,
"I will have mercy on whom I have mercy, and I will
    have compassion on whom I have compassion."
So it depends not on human will or exertion, but on God who shows mercy.

ROMANS 9:15–16

Mercy

Jesus said, "Be merciful, just as your father is merciful."

LUKE 6:36

The Lord never withdraws his mercy from us.
Although he disciplines us with calamities, he does not
forsake his own people.

2 MACCABEES 6:16

Judgment will be without mercy to anyone who has
shown no mercy, mercy triumphs over judgment.

JAMES 2:13

Keep yourselves in the love of God; look forward to the
mercy of our Lord Jesus Christ that leads to eternal
life. And have mercy on some who are wavering; save
others by snatching them out of the fire; and have
mercy on still others with fear.

JUDE 21–22

Because the LORD your God is a merciful God, he
will neither abandon you nor destroy you; he will not
forget the covenant with your ancestors that he swore
to them.

DEUTERONOMY 4:31

Be merciful to me, O God, be merciful to me,
    for in you my soul takes refuge;
in the shadow of your wings I will take refuge,
    until the destroying storms pass by.

PSALM 57:1

Mercy

Have mercy on me, O God,
according to your steadfast love;
according to your abundant mercy
blot out my transgressions.
Wash me thoroughly from my iniquity,
and cleanse me from my sin.

PSALM 51:1–2

Answer me, O LORD, for you steadfast love is good;
according to your abundant mercy, turn to me.

PSALM 69:16

God, who is rich in mercy, out of the great love with
which he loved us even when we were dead through
our trespasses, made us alive together with Christ.

EPHESIANS 2:4–5

The Mighty One has done great things for me,
and holy is his name.
His mercy is for those who fear him
from generation to generation.

LUKE 1:49–50

Do not, O LORD, withhold
your mercy from me;
let your steadfast love and your faithfulness
keep me safe forever.

PSALM 40:11

*O*ne day one of my roommates asked to borrow my car. It was raining hard and I was afraid both for her safety and for my car. I told her that I'd prefer she wait. But she felt it was important to go immediately.

I was eating dinner when she returned looking very ashamed. "Patti, I got in a wreck on the bridge, and your car had to be towed away."

In a flash I knew what mercy was. In my mind's eye I could see myself getting up from the table and embracing her with the words, "Thank God you weren't hurt. It's all right. Don't worry about it." But reason quickly intervened. I looked at her sullenly and mumbled, "I told you it wasn't the best time to go."

Meekly she left the room. There I sat, knowing I had missed an opportunity to be merciful as my heavenly Father is merciful. In that moment, the merciful thing would have been to console her.

His ways are not our ways. His thoughts are not our thoughts. Mercy will never "make sense" or "seem reasonable." We can rejoice that our Lord never gives us what we truly deserve.

Patti Gallagher Mansfield

Peace

O LORD, you will ordain peace for us,
    for indeed, all that we have done, you have done
    for us.

ISAIAH 26:12

*Christ is our peace; in his flesh he has made both
groups into one and has broken down the dividing
wall, that is, the hostility between us.*

EPHESIANS 2:14

My children, be true to your training and be at peace.

SIRACH 41:14

You shall go out in joy,
    and be led back in peace;
the mountains and the hills before you
        shall burst into song,
        and all the trees of the field shall clap their hands.

ISAIAH 55:12

*Christ came and proclaimed peace to you who were
far off and peace to those who were near; for through
him both of us have access in one Spirit to the Father.*

EPHESIANS 2:17–18

Depart from evil, and do good;
    seek peace, and pursue it.

PSALM 34:14

Peace

I will both lie down and sleep in peace;
  for you alone, O LORD, make me lie down in safety.

PSALM 4:8

*The peace of God, which surpasses all understanding
will guard your hearts and your minds in Christ Jesus.*

PHILIPPIANS 4:7

*Let the peace of Christ rule in your hearts, to which
indeed you were called in the one body. And be thankful.*

COLOSSIANS 3:15

Deceit is in the mind of those who plan evil,
  but those who counsel peace have joy.

PROVERBS 12:20

*Shun youthful passions and pursue righteousness,
faith, love, and peace, along with those who call on the
Lord from a pure heart.*

2 TIMOTHY 2:22

When the ways of people please the LORD,
  he causes even their enemies to be at peace with
  them.

PROVERBS 16:7

*Let us then pursue what makes for peace and for
mutual upbuilding.*

ROMANS 14:19

Peace

If it is possible, so far as it depends on you, live peaceably with all.

ROMANS 12:18

Grace to you and peace from God our Father and the Lord Jesus Christ.

PHILIPPIANS 1:2

How beautiful upon the mountains
are the feet of the messenger who announces peace,
who brings good news,
who announces salvation,
who says to Zion, "Your God reigns."

ISAIAH 52:7

Agree with God, and be at peace;
in this way good will come to you.

JOB 22:21

Great peace have those who love your law;
nothing can make them stumble.

PSALM 119:165

Peace, peace, to the far and the near, says the LORD;
and I will heal them.

ISAIAH 57:19

*P*eace

Let me hear what God the LORD will speak,
    for he will speak peace to his people,
    to his faithful, to those who turn to him in their
    hearts. ...
Steadfast love and faithfulness will meet;
    righteousness and peace will kiss each other.

PSALM 85:8,10

A child has been born for us,
    a son given to us;
authority rests upon his shoulders,
    and he is named
Wonderful Counselor, Mighty God,
    Everlasting Father, Prince of Peace.
His authority shall grow continually,
    and there shall be endless peace
for the throne of David and his kingdom.
    He will establish and uphold it
with justice and with righteousness
    from this time onward and forevermore.
The zeal of the LORD of hosts will do this.

ISAIAH 9:6-7

*May the Lord of peace himself give you peace at all
times in all ways. The Lord be with all of you.*

2 THESSALONIANS 3:16

*P*eace

Keep on doing the things that you have learned and received and heard and seen in me and the God of peace will be with you.

PHILIPPIANS 4:9

To set the mind on the flesh is death, but to set the mind on the Spirit is life and peace.

ROMANS 8:6

Jesus said, "Blessed are the peacemakers, for they will be called children of God."

MATTHEW 5:9

Jesus said, "Peace I leave with you; my peace I give to you. I do not give to you as the world gives. Do not let your hearts be troubled, and do not let them be afraid."

JOHN 14:27

The wisdom from above is first pure, then peaceable, gentle, willing to yield, full of mercy and good fruits, without a trace of partiality or hypocrisy. And a harvest of righteousness is sown in peace for those who make peace.

JAMES 3:17–18

*W*henever I am worried, I say the 23rd Psalm. This truly gives me "the peace of God which surpasses all understanding" (Philippians 4:7).

My most dramatic experience of this was on a recent flight to Dallas, Texas. Shortly after departure the pilot announced that bad storms were ahead. Soon lightning was flashing, thunder was crashing, and the plane was really being tossed about. I closed my eyes and concentrated on Psalm 23.

Next thing I knew, we were on the ground. That's when I learned how rough the ride had been. We had almost landed in Dallas when the pilot was told to pull up and head for Austin. Then, while doing this, he was instructed to return and land immediately, as tornadoes had been sighted. Apparently, this abrupt shifting of direction caused quite a disturbance in the cabin!

But guess what? I had missed it all. The Lord in his kindness had put me to sleep—he must have, as I knew nothing about any of this! What could have been a very fearful experience was nothing more than a quick snooze. I trusted God, and he took care of the situation and took away my fear!

Hazel Miller

$\mathcal{P}$rayer

Jesus said, "Ask, and it will be given you; search and you will find; knock, and the door will be opened for you. For everyone who asks receives, and everyone who searches finds, and for everyone who knocks, the door will be opened."

MATTHEW 7:7–8

The prayer of the poor goes from their lips to the ears of God,
>   and his judgment comes speedily.

SIRACH 21:5

Are any among you suffering? They should pray. Are any cheerful? They should sing songs of praise. Are any among you sick? They should call for the elders of the church and have them pray over them, anointing them with oil in the name of the Lord. The prayer of faith will save the sick, and the Lord will raise them up; and anyone who has committed sins will be forgiven. Therefore confess your sins to one another, and pray for one another, so that you may be healed. The prayer of the righteous is powerful and effective.

JAMES 5:13–16

Give ear, O LORD, to my prayer;
>   listen to my cry of supplication.
In the day of my trouble I all on you,
>   for you will answer me.

PSALM 86:6–7

....

*P*rayer

The Spirit helps us in our weakness; for we do not know how to pray as we ought, but that very Spirit intercedes with sighs too deep for words.

ROMANS 8:26

The LORD is far from the wicked,
     but he hears the prayer of the righteous.

PROVERBS 15:29

Jesus said, "Whenever you pray, go into your room and shut the door and pray to your Father who is in secret; and your Father who sees in secret will reward you."

MATTHEW 6:6

Call to me and I will answer you, and will tell you great and hidden things that you have not known.

JEREMIAH 33:3

Jesus said, "I will do whatever you ask in my name, so that the Father may be glorified in the Son. If in my name you ask me for anything, I will do it."

JOHN 14:13–14

Do not grow weary when you pray;
     do not neglect to give alms.

SIRACH 7:10

....

$\mathcal{P}$rayer

Therefore let all who are faithful
> offer prayer to you;
at a time of distress, the rush of mighty waters
> shall not reach them.

PSALM 32:6

Beloved, if our hearts do not condemn us, we have
boldness before God; and we receive from him
whatever we ask, because we obey his commandments
and do what pleases him.

1 JOHN 3:21–22

Jesus said, "If you abide in me, and my words abide
in you, ask for whatever you wish, and it will be done
for you."

JOHN 15:7

At that very moment, the prayers of both of them were
heard in the glorious presence of God.

TOBIT 3:16

Hear a just cause, O LORD; attend to my cry;
> give ear to my prayer from lips free of deceit.

PSALM 17:1

When you call upon me and come and pray to me, I
will hear you. When you search for me, you will find
me; if you seek me with all your heart, says the LORD.

JEREMIAH 29:12–13

*P*rayer

Before they call I will answer,
    while they are yet speaking I will hear.

ISAIAH 65:24

*Pray in the Spirit at all times in every prayer and
supplication. To that end keep alert and always
persevere in supplication for all the saints.*

EPHESIANS 6:18

Answer me when I call, O God of my right!
    You gave me room when I was in distress.
    Be gracious to me, and hear my prayer. ...
But know that the LORD has set apart the faithful for
himself;
    the LORD hears when I call to him.

PSALM 4:1,3

Rejoice always, pray without ceasing.

1 THESSALONIANS 5:16–17

For the eyes of the Lord are on the righteous,
    and his ears are open to their prayer.
But the face of the Lord is against
    those who do evil.

1 PETER 3:12

*Do not worry about anything, but in everything by
prayer and supplication with thanksgiving let your
requests be made known to God.*

PHILIPPIANS 4:6

*P*rayer

I called to the LORD out of my distress,
and he answered me.

JONAH 2:2

*Jesus said, "Whatever you ask for in prayer, believe
that you have received it, and it will be yours."*

MARK 11:24

Hear, O Lord, the prayer of your servants,
according to your goodwill toward your people,
and all who are on the earth will know
that you are the Lord, the God of the ages.

SIRACH 36:22

*Everything created by God is good, and nothing is to
be rejected, provided it is received with thanksgiving;
for it is sanctified by God's word and by prayer.*

1 TIMOTHY 4:4–5

I call upon you, O LORD; come quickly to me;
give ear to my voice when I call to you.
Let my prayer be counted as incense before you,
and the lifting up of my hands as an evening sacrifice.

PSALM 141:1–2

*I*t is one of my favorite morning rituals. I begin my day with a cup of tea or coffee. As the steam from my cup ascends to the heavens, I walk with all my favorite strangers into the heart of God. There is a bit of the stranger in everyone—even friends.

I yearn for God to bless all the peoples of the earth. And so I name my friends to God. Sometimes I do not even name them. I simply see their faces in the ascending steam. Often the faces of people whose names I don't even know come to me: people at checkout counters in the stores, folks I've seen during my travels, in the airport, or on the streets. There are the faces of those I read about in the newspapers or seen in the evening news. All are strangers. All are friends.

The reason I like my Prayer of the Teacup is that it is so simple. I believe that when we pray for others, we often get bogged down with words. I need few words—just a name or a glance is enough. I simply look at these strangers and friends whom God loves, and I yearn for their good.

Macrina Wiederkehr

*P*ride

Some take pride in chariots, and some in horses,
    but our pride is in the name of the LORD our God.
They will collapse and fall,
    but we shall rise and stand upright.

PSALM 20:7–8

Do not love the world or the things in the world. The love of the Father is not in those who love the world, for all that is in the world—the desire of the flesh, the desire of the eyes, the pride in riches—comes not from the Father but from the world. And the world and its desire are passing away, but those who do the will of God live forever.

1 JOHN 2:15–17

When pride comes, then comes disgrace; but wisdom is with the humble.

PROVERBS 11:2

He gives all the more grace; therefore it says,
    "God opposes the proud,
        but gives grace to the humble."

JAMES 4:6

Pride goes before destruction,
    and a haughty spirit before a fall.

PROVERBS 16:18

$\mathscr{P}$ride

Better is the end of a thing than its beginning;
the patient in spirit are better than the proud in
spirit.

ECCLESIASTES 7:8

Though the LORD is high, he regards the lowly;
but the haughty he perceives from far away.

PSALM 138:6

The haughty eyes of people shall be brought low,
and the pride of everyone shall be humbled;
and the LORD alone will be exalted on that day.
For the LORD of hosts has a day
against all that is proud and lofty,
against all that is lifted up and high.

ISAIAH 2:11–12

I, wisdom, live with prudence,
and I attain knowledge and discretion.
The fear of the Lord is hatred of evil.
Pride and arrogance and the way of evil
and perverted speech I hate.

PROVERBS 8:12–13

Jesus said, "All who exalt themselves will be humbled,
but all who humble themselves will be exalted."

LUKE 18:14

$\mathcal{P}$ride

The beginning of human pride is to forsake the Lord;
the heart has withdrawn from its Maker.
For the beginning of pride is sin,
and the one who clings to it pours out abominations.
Therefore the Lord brings upon them unheard-of
calamities,
and destroys them completely.

SIRACH 10:12–13

A person's pride will bring humiliation,
but one who is lowly in spirit will obtain honor.

PROVERBS 29:23

*Thus says the LORD: Do not let the wise boast in their
wisdom, do not let the mighty boast in their might, do
not let the wealthy boast in their wealth, but let those
who boast, boast in this, that they understand and
know me, that I am the LORD; I act with steadfast
love, justice, and righteousness in the earth, for in these
things I delight, says the LORD.*

JEREMIAH 9:23–24

Praise and extol and honor the King of heaven,
for all his works are truth, and his ways are justice;
and he is able to bring low those who walk in pride.

DANIEL 4:37

*M*uch as we want to know ourselves, we do not really know ourselves. Do we really want to see ourselves as God sees us, or even as our fellow human beings see us? Could we bear it, weak as we are?

You know that feeling of contentment in which we sometimes go about, clothed in it as it were, like a garment, content with the world and with ourselves. We are ourselves and we would be no one else. We are glad that God made us as we are and we would not have had him make us like anyone else. According to the weather, our state of health, we have moods of purely animal happiness and contentment. We do not want to be given that clear inward vision which discloses to us our most secret faults.

In the psalms there is that prayer, "Clear me from hidden faults." We do not really know how much pride and self-love we have until someone whom we respect or love suddenly turns against us. Then some sudden affront, some sudden offense we take, reveals to us in all its glaring distinctness our self-love, and we are ashamed.

Dorothy Day

*P*riorities

Happy are those
 who do not follow the advice of the wicked,
or take the path that sinners tread,
 or sit in the seat of scoffers;
but their delight is in the law of the LORD,
 and on his law they meditate day and night.
They are like trees
 planted by streams of water,
which yield their fruit in its season,
 and their leaves do not wither.
In all that they do, they prosper.

PSALM 1:1–3

Become... imitators of those who through faith and patience inherit the promises.

HEBREWS 6:12

Live you life in a manner worthy of the gospel of Christ, so that whether I come and see you or am absent and hear about you, I will know that you are standing firm in one spirit, striving side by side with one mind for the faith of the gospel, and are in no way intimidated by your opponents.

PHILIPPIANS 1:27–28

Someone will say, "You have faith and I have works." Show me your faith apart from your works, and I by my works will show you my faith.

JAMES 2:18

$\mathcal{P}$riorities

I press on toward the goal for the prize of the heavenly call of God in Christ Jesus.

PHILIPPIANS 3:14

Take good care to observe the commandment and instruction that Moses the servant of the LORD commanded you, to love the LORD your God, to walk in all his ways, to keep his commandments, and to hold fast to him, and to serve him with all your heart and with all your soul.

JOSHUA 22:5

Jesus said, "Do not worry, saying, 'What will we eat?' or 'What will we drink?' or 'What will we wear?' For it is the Gentiles who strive for all these things; and indeed your heavenly Father knows that you need all these things. But strive first for the kingdom of God and his righteousness, and all these things will be given to you as well."

MATTHEW 6:31–33

We look not at what can be seen but at what cannot be seen; for what can be seen is temporary, but what cannot be seen is eternal.

2 CORINTHIANS 4:18

*P*riorities

If you have been raised with Christ, seek the things that are above, where Christ is, seated at the right hand of God. Set your minds on things that are above, not on things that are on earth, for you have died, and your life is hidden with Christ in God.

COLOSSIANS 3:1–3

I call heaven and earth to witness against you today that I have set before you life and death, blessings and curses. Choose life so that you and your descendants may live, loving the LORD your God, obeying him, and holding fast to him; for that means life to you.

DEUTERONOMY 30:19–20

Take delight in the LORD,
    and he will give you the desires of your heart.

PSALM 37:4

Be of the same mind, having the same love, being in full accord and of one mind. Do nothing from selfish ambition or conceit, but in humility regard others as better than yourselves. Let each of you look not to your own interests, but to the interests of others. Let the same mind be in you that was in Christ Jesus.

PHILIPPIANS 2:2–5

Priorities

Choose this day whom you will serve, whether the gods your ancestors served in the region beyond the River or the gods of the Amorites in whose land you are living; but as for me and my household, we will serve the LORD.

JOSHUA 24:15

Jesus said, "Blessed are those who hunger and thirst for righteousness, for they will be filled."

MATTHEW 5:6

Jesus said, "Do not work for the food that perishes, but for the food that endures for eternal life, which the Son of Man will give you. For it is on him that God the Father has set his seal."

JOHN 6:27

Put away from you crooked speech,
    and put devious talk far from you.
Let your eyes look directly forward,
    and your gaze be straight before you.
Keep straight the path of your feet,
    and all your ways will be sure.
Do not swerve to the right or to the left;
    turn your foot away from evil.

PROVERBS 4:24–27

*P*riorities

Since we are surrounded by so great a cloud of witnesses, let us also lay aside every weight and the sin that clings so closely, and let us run with perseverance the race that is set before us, looking to Jesus the pioneer and perfecter of our faith, who for the sake of the joy that was set before him endured the cross, disregarding its shame, and has taken his seat at the right hand of the throne of God.

HEBREWS 12:1–2

I have chosen the way of faithfulness;
　　I set your ordinances before me.
I cling to your decrees, O LORD;
　　let me not be put to shame.

PSALM 119:30–31

You who fear the Lord, wait for his mercy;
　　do not stray, or else you may fall.
You who fear the Lord, trust in him,
　　and your reward will not be lost.
You who fear the Lord, hope for good things,
　　for lasting joy and mercy.

SIRACH 2:7–9

Have nothing to do with profane myths and old wives' tales. Train yourself in godliness, for, while physical training is of some value, godliness is valuable in every way, holding promise for both the present life and the life to come.

1 TIMOTHY 4:7–8

*W*omen are called to use their time wisely, just as men are. This means we must defy the way the "world" values time. The world thinks that time spent in prayer and silent communion with God is time wasted. But Jesus in his call to Martha and his affirmation of Mary countered this: Time spent in touch with him, growing in faith, is of crucial importance. The world tells us that our most important time is time spent earning money. Women tend to earn less money, so their time is worth less than men's time, a valuation that does not come from God but from the world. All disciples are to make "the most of the time."

To assume the biblical stance that all are called equally to follow God, to use their time and talents for him and to exercise their callings based on gifts, we have to fight a wealth of cultural biases that tell women their time is cheap and their callings trivial. When a woman begins to sense herself called by Jesus, she may begin to claim the time to do what she needs to do. It may be spent in prayer, in caring for a dying parent, in writing, in going to medical school.

Mary Ellen Ashcroft

Rest

I lie down and sleep; I wake again,
for the LORD sustains me.

PSALM 3:5

*On the seventh day God finished the work that he
had done, and he rested on the seventh day from all
the work that he had done. So God blessed the seventh
day and hallowed it, because on it God rested from
all the work that he had done in creation.*

GENESIS 2:1–3

I keep the LORD always before me;
because he is at my right hand, I shall not be moved.
Therefore my heart is glad, and my soul rejoices;
my body also rests secure.

PSALM 16:8–9

The LORD is my shepherd, I shall not want.
He makes me lie down in green pastures;
he leads me beside still waters;
he restores my soul.
He leads me in right paths for his name's sake.

PSALM 23:1–3

*Jesus said, "Come away to a deserted place all by
yourselves and rest a while."*

MARK 6:31

Rest

I will recount the gracious deeds of the LORD,
    the praiseworthy acts of the LORD,
because of all that the LORD has done for us,
    and the great favor to the house of Israel
that he has shown them according to his mercy,
    according to the abundance of his steadfast love. ...
Like cattle that go down into the valley,
    the spirit of the Lord gave them rest.

ISAIAH 63:7,14

Sweet is the sleep of laborers, whether they eat little or much; but the surfeit of the rich will not let them sleep.

ECCLESIASTES 5:12

Thus says the LORD of hosts, the God of Israel: ...
I will satisfy the weary,
    and all who are faint I will replenish.

JEREMIAH 31:23,25

The beloved of the LORD rests in safety—
    the High God surrounds him all day long—
    the beloved rests between his shoulders.

DEUTERONOMY 33:12

You will have confidence, because there is hope;
you will be protected and take your rest in safety.

JOB 11:18

Rest

Jesus said, "Come to me, all you that are weary and are carrying heavy burdens, and I will give you rest. Take my yoke upon you, and learn from me; for I am gentle and humble in heart, and you will find rest for your souls. For my yoke is easy, and my burden is light."

MATTHEW 11:28–30

Blessed be the LORD, who has given rest to his people Israel according to all that he promised; not one word has failed of all his good promises, which he spoke through his servant Moses.

1 KINGS 8:56

Remember the Sabbath day, and keep it holy. Six days you shall labor and do all your work. ... For in six days the LORD made heaven and earth, the sea, and all that is in them, but rested the seventh day; therefore the LORD blessed the Sabbath day and consecrated it.

EXODUS 20:8–9,11

A Sabbath rest still remains for the people of God; for those who enter God's rest also cease from their labors as God did from his. Let us therefore make every effort to enter that rest, so that no one may fall.

HEBREWS 4:9–11

Rest

Thus says the LORD:
Stand at the crossroads, and look,
    and ask for the ancient paths,
where the good way lies; and walk in it,
    and find rest for your souls.

JEREMIAH 6:16

I will give you rest from all your enemies.

2 SAMUEL 7:11

Trust in the LORD, and do good;
    so you will live in the land and enjoy security.

PSALM 37:3

If you sit down, you will not be afraid,
    when you lie down, your sleep will be sweet.
Do not be afraid of sudden panic,
    or of the storm that strikes the wicked;
for the LORD will be your confidence
    and will keep your foot from being caught.

PROVERBS 3:24–26

You who live in the shelter of the Most High,
    who abide in the shadow of the Almighty,
will say to the LORD, "My refuge and my fortress;
    my God, in whom I trust."

PSALM 91:1–2

Rest

The LORD said, "My presence will go with you, and I will give you rest."

EXODUS 33:14

Thus said the Lord GOD, the Holy One of Israel:
In returning and rest you shall be saved;
  in quietness and in trust shall be your strength.

ISAIAH 30:15

Gracious is the LORD, and righteous;
  our God is merciful.
The LORD protects the simple;
  when I was brought low, he saved me.
Return, O my soul, to your rest,
  for the LORD has dealt bountifully with you.

PSALM 116:5–7

My people will abide in a peaceful habitation,
  in secure dwellings, and in quiet resting places.

ISAIAH 32:18

O LORD, my heart is not lifted up,
  my eyes are not raised too high;
I do not occupy myself with things
  too great and too marvelous for me.
But I have calmed and quieted my soul,
  like a weaned child with its mother;
    my soul is like the weaned child that is with me.

PSALM 131:1–2

"*C*ome to me," cries Jesus. "I will give you rest." I don't know about you, but for me, to speak of eternal joy, delight, bliss, is unreal. I simply cannot imagine unalloyed joy and delight engulfing the whole of me. I know joy, but it is that of sacrifice, of loving God at cost, this is the only joy that means anything to me. But when I think of the more modest term rest— yes, then my heart responds.

To be at rest; yearning, struggle, empty longing filled … yes, that means something. I will give you rest because I give you the Father, and you come to me by taking my yoke upon yourself, the yoke of humble, meek, devoted loving. This is to know the Father, the God of all compassion.

Ruth Burrows

Strength

Your strength, O God, does not depend on numbers, nor your might on the powerful. But you are the God of the lowly, helper of the oppressed, upholder of the weak, protector of the forsaken, savior of those without hope.

JUDITH 9:11

I love you, O LORD, my strength,
The LORD is my rock, my fortress, and my deliverer,
    my God, my rock in whom I take refuge;
    my shield, and the horn of my salvation, my
    stronghold.

PSALM 18:1–2

To him who by the power at work within us is able to accomplish abundantly far more than all we can ask or imagine, to him be glory in the church and in Christ Jesus to all generations, forever and ever, Amen.

EPHESIANS 3:20–21

My soul melts away from sorrow;
    strengthen me according to your word.

PSALM 119:28

The Lord stood by me and gave me strength, so that through me the message might be fully proclaimed and all the Gentiles might hear it.

2 TIMOTHY 4:17

Strength

Riches and honor come from you, and you rule over all. In your hand are power and might; and it is in your hand to make great and to give strength to all. And now, our God, we give thanks to you and praise your glorious name.

1 CHRONICLES 29:12–13

It is not on the size of the army that victory in battle depends, but strength comes from Heaven.

1 MACCABEES 3:19

Be strong in the Lord and in the strength of his power.

EPHESIANS 6:10

God is our refuge and strength,
    a very present help in trouble.
Therefore we will not fear, though the earth should change,
    though the mountains shake in the heart of the sea;
though its waters roar and foam,
    though the mountains tremble with its tumult.

PSALM 46:1–3

Surely God is my salvation;
    I will trust, and will not be afraid,
for the LORD GOD is my strength and my might;
    he has become my salvation.

ISAIAH 12:2

Strength

He said to me, "My grace is sufficient for you, for power is made perfect in weakness." So, I will boast all the more gladly of my weaknesses, so that the power of Christ may dwell in me. Therefore I am content with weaknesses, insults, hardships, persecutions, and calamities for the sake of Christ; for whenever I am weak, then I am strong.

2 CORINTHIANS 12:9–10

The LORD is the everlasting God,
     the Creator of the ends of the earth.
He does not faint or grow weary;
     his understanding is unsearchable.
He gives power to the faint,
     and strengthens the powerless.

ISAIAH 40:28–29

God's foolishness is wiser than human wisdom, and God's weakness is stronger than human strength.

1 CORINTHIANS 1:25

I can do all things through him who strengthens me.

PHILIPPIANS 4:13

May you be made strong with all the strength that comes from his glorious power, and may you be prepared to endure everything with patience, while joyfully giving thanks to the Father.

COLOSSIANS 1:11–12

Strength

Do not be grieved, for the joy of the LORD *is your strength.*

NEHEMIAH 8:10

The LORD is my strength and my shield;
in him my heart trusts;
so I am helped, and my heart exults,
and with my song I give thanks to him.

PSALM 28:7

May the LORD give strength to his people!
May the LORD bless his people with peace!

PSALM 29:11

I pray that, according to the riches of his glory, he may grant that you may be strengthened in your inner being with power through his Spirit, and that Christ may dwell in your hearts through faith, as you are being rooted and grounded in love.

EPHESIANS 3:16–17

My flesh and my heart may fail,
but God is the strength of my heart and my
portion forever.

PSALM 73:26

Strength

*With the eyes of your heart enlightened, you may
know what is the hope to which he has called you,
what are the riches of his glorious inheritance among
the saints, and what is the immeasurable greatness of
his power for us who believe, according to the working
of his great power.*

EPHESIANS 1:18–19

Awesome is God in his sanctuary,
    the God of Israel;
    he gives power and strength to his people.
Blessed be God!

PSALM 68:35

*The eyes of the LORD range throughout the entire
earth, to strengthen those whose heart is true to him.*

2 CHRONICLES 16:9

*Ah, Lord GOD! It is you who made the heavens and
the earth by your great power and by your outstretched
arm! Nothing is too hard for you.*

JEREMIAH 32:17

*T*he book of Judith illustrates for every age the source and availability of true power. Judith makes preparation for her task as the instrument of God's victory. Her primary preparation is prayer. Her attitude of prayer demonstrates her faith in the absolute supremacy of God. However, [it] is not a statement of weakness but a request to be filled with the power of God. Judith's subsequent activity is the preparation of the weapons given her by God. She will not win the victory with horses and chariots but rather with beauty and wit, gifts from the God in whose power she acts.

Judith stands as companion to other women of God: women who look not to themselves for power and strength but who place their trust completely in God; women who are strong enough in faith to allow God to be free and strong enough to wait for God's good time; women who cannot be defeated by despair. This is the model, the strong and faithful woman of God, which the author of the book of Judith presents to the Jewish people, threatened by world powers and bearing the weight of persecution. This same model may well give courage and direction to our own age.

Irene Nowell, O.S.B.

Time with God

Reflect on the statutes of the Lord,
    and meditate at all times on his commandments.
It is he who will give insight to your mind,
    and your desire for wisdom will be granted.

SIRACH 6:37

Hear, O LORD, when I cry aloud,
    be gracious to me and answer me!
"Come," my heart says, "seek his face!"
    Your face, LORD, do I seek.
    Do not hide your face from me.

PSALM 27:7–9

The LORD is in his holy temple;
    let all the earth keep silence before him!

HABAKKUK 2:20

O God, you are my God, I seek you,
    my soul thirsts for you;
my flesh faints for you,
    as in a dry and weary land where there is no water. ...
My soul is satisfied as with a rich feast,
    and my mouth praises you with joyful lips
when I think of you on my bed,
    and meditate on you in the watches of the night;
for you have been my help
    and in the shadow of your wings I sing for joy.

PSALM 63:1,5–7

Time with God

Without faith it is impossible to please God, for whoever would approach him must believe that he exists and that he rewards those who seek him.

HEBREWS 11:6

Listen! I am standing at the door, knocking; if you hear my voice and open the door, I will come in to you and eat with you, and you with me.

REVELATION 3:20

One thing I asked of the LORD,
    that will I seek after;
to live in the house of the LORD
    all the days of my life,
to behold the beauty of the LORD,
    and to inquire in his temple.

PSALM 27:4

Although Daniel knew that the document had been signed, he continued to go to his house, which had windows in its upper room open toward Jerusalem, and to get down on his knees three times a day to pray to his God and praise him, just as he had done previously.

DANIEL 6:10

We have access to God in boldness and confidence through faith in him.

EPHESIANS 3:12

Time with God

Seek the LORD while he may be found,
    call upon him while he is near;
let the wicked forsake their way,
    and the unrighteous their thoughts;
let them return to the Lord, that he may have mercy
on them,
    and to our God, for he will abundantly pardon.

ISAIAH 55:6–7

Draw near to God, and he will draw near to you.

JAMES 4:8

The LORD is with you, while you are with him. If you seek him, he will be found by you, but if you abandon him, he will abandon you.

2 CHRONICLES 15:2

Create in me a clean heart, O God,
    and put a new and right spirit within me.
Do not cast me away from your presence
    and do not take your holy spirit from me.
Restore to me the joy of your salvation,
    and sustain in me a willing spirit.

PSALM 51:10–12

I bless the LORD who gives me counsel;
    in the night also my heart instructs me.
I keep the LORD always before me;
    because he is at my right hand, I shall not be moved.

PSALM 16:7–8

I'd like to share a teaching that came to me one day as I sat before the Lord. I was just looking at the Blessed Sacrament and adoring Jesus and telling him I didn't have much to say except that I loved him.

I felt as though the Lord said to me, "Well, don't you know that you don't have to say anything to me? Just be with me. Come into my presence. It's not what you do for me, it's what I want to do for you."

Then I got an image of a person going out of his house and sitting in the sun. As he sat in the sun, he didn't do a thing, but he started to change color. People who saw him knew he had been in the sun because his skin showed it. The man knew it, too, because he felt the effects of the sun: the warmth and the light.

I heard the Lord saying, "So it is when you come into my presence. You will experience the effects of your time spent with me. People will see it in your actions."

It was a great teaching to me, knowing that I didn't always have to be saying things, but all I had to do was be there with Jesus.

Briege McKenna, O.S.C.

Trust

Blessed are those who trust in the LORD,
>   whose trust is the Lord,
They shall be like a tree planted by water,
>   sending out its roots by the stream.
It shall not fear when heat comes,
>   and its leaves shall stay green;
in the year of drought it is not anxious
>   and it does not cease to bear fruit.

JEREMIAH 17:7–8

Trust in the Lord, and he will help you;
>   make your ways straight and hope in him

SIRACH 2:6

Daniel was taken up out of the den, and no kind of harm was found on him, because he had trusted in his God.

DANIEL 6:23

Trust in the LORD with all your heart,
>   and do not rely on your own insight.
In all your ways acknowledge him,
>   and he will make straight you paths.

PROVERBS 3:5–6

Trust

O Most High, when I am afraid,
    I put my trust in you.
In God, whose word I praise,
    in God I trust; I am not afraid;
    what can flesh do to me?

PSALM 56:3–4

I trust in your steadfast love;
    my heart shall rejoice in your salvation.
I will sing to the LORD,
    because he has dealt bountifully with me.

PSALM 13:5–6

Those who trust in God will understand truth,
and the faithful will abide with him in love,
because grace and mercy are upon his holy ones
and he watches over his elect.

THE WISDOM OF SOLOMON 3:9

One who trusts in the LORD is secure.

PROVERBS 29:25

O LORD of hosts
    happy is everyone who trusts in you.

PSALM 84:12

Trust

Those of steadfast mind you keep in peace—
in peace because they trust in you.
Trust in the LORD forever,
for in the LORD God
you have an everlasting rock.

ISAIAH 26:3–4

*Hezekiah trusted in the Lord the God of Israel; so
that there was no one like him among all the kings of
Judah after him, or among those who were before
him. For he held fast to the LORD; he did not depart
from following him but kept the commandments that
the Lord commanded Moses. The LORD was with
him; wherever he went, he prospered.*

2 KINGS 18:5–7

Many are the torments of the wicked,
but steadfast love surrounds those who trust in
the LORD.

PSALM 32:10

Those who are attentive to a matter will prosper,
and happy are those who trust in the LORD.

PROVERBS 16:20

Those who know your name put their trust in you,
for you, O LORD, have not forsaken those who
seek you.

PSALM 9:10

Trust

The greedy person stirs up strife,
>but whoever trusts in the LORD will be enriched.

>PROVERBS 28:25

Our soul waits for the LORD;
>he is our help and shield.

Our heart is glad in him,
>because we trust in his holy name.

Let your steadfast love, O LORD, be upon us,
>even as we hope in you.

>PSALM 33:20–22

Happy are those who make
>the LORD their trust,

who do not turn to the proud,
>to those who go astray after false gods.

>PSALM 40:4

But I trust in you, O LORD;
>I say, "You are my God."

My times are in your hand;
>deliver me from the hand of my enemies and
>persecutors.

Let your face shine upon your servant;
>save me in your steadfast love.

>PSALM 31:14–16

*T*rust

Trust in him at all times, O people;
>pour out your heart before him;
>God is a refuge for us.

PSALM 62:8

The LORD is on my side to help me;
>I shall look in triumph on those who hate me.
It is better to take refuge in the LORD
>than to put confidence in mortals.
It is better to take refuge in the LORD
>than to put confidence in princes.

PSALM 118:7–9

Those who trust in the LORD are like Mount Zion,
>which cannot be moved, but abides forever. ...
Do good, O LORD, to those who are good,
>and to those who are upright in their hearts.

PSALM 125:1,4

To you, O LORD, I lift up my soul.
O my God, in you I trust;
>do not let me be put to shame;
>do not let my enemies exult over me.

PSALM 25:1–2

Let me hear of your steadfast love in the morning,
>for in you I put my trust.
Teach me the way I should go,
>for to you I lift up my soul.

PSALM 143:8

To trust God means that we must know that whatever comes to us comes from his hand. If we do not see that sorrow comes from his hand and cannot get the comfort of his love from it, it may be because we do not acknowledge our joys as his gifts. If we felt grateful for our food, for the sunlight, for our work, our homes, for those we love, if we were conscious that these were all given by God, we should have formed a clear enough idea of his love to know that he does not want us to suffer, but allows it because there is good for us in it. To resist, to be bitter increases the pain. To accept it gratefully from God eases the pain.

Make a mental picture of two huge giving hands. God's hands, and every so often stop and think: "At this moment, God is handing me all I have," mentioning all that you are conscious of. At some moments you will realize what a lot of obvious good God is giving you. Still at other times, it will help you to understand that the trials you suffer also come from his hands.

Caryll Houselander

Waiting

I wait for the LORD, my soul waits,
>   and in his word I hope;
my soul waits for the Lord
>   more than those who watch for the morning.

PSALM 130:5–6

*In accordance with his promise, we wait for new heavens
and a new earth, where righteousness is at home.*

2 PETER 3:13

Those who are patient stay calm until the right moment,
>   and then cheerfulness comes back to them.

SIRACH 1:23

Be still before the LORD, and wait patiently for him;
>   do not fret over those who prosper in their way,
>   over those who carry out evil devices.

PSALM 37:7

The LORD is good to those who wait for him,
>   to the soul that seeks him.
It is good that one should wait quietly
>   for the salvation of the LORD.

LAMENTATIONS 3:25–26

*The testing of your faith produces endurance; and let
endurance have its full effect, so that you may be
mature and complete, lacking in nothing.*

JAMES 1:3–4

*W*aiting

You who fear the Lord, wait for his mercy;
    do not stray, or else you may fall.

Sirach 2:7

I believe that I shall see the goodness of the Lord
    in the land of the living.
Wait for the Lord;
    be strong, and let your heart take courage;
    wait for the Lord!

Psalm 27:13–14

*Be patient, therefore, beloved, until the coming of the
Lord. The farmer waits for the precious crop from the
earth, being patient with it until it receives the early
and the late rains. You also must be patient. Strengthen
your hearts, for the coming of the Lord is near.*

James 5:7–8

*If we hope for what we do not see, we wait for it
with patience.*

Romans 8:25

*Do not, therefore, abandon that confidence of yours; it
brings a great reward. For you need endurance, so
that when you have done the will of God, you may
receive what was promised.*

Hebrews 10:35-36

*W*aiting

Jesus said, "The one who endures to the end will be saved."

MATTHEW 24:13

In the path of your judgments,
    O LORD, we wait for you;
your name and your renown
    are the soul's desire.

ISAIAH 26:8

I waited patiently for the LORD;
    he inclined to me and heard my cry. ...
He put a new song in my mouth,
    a song of praise to our God.
Many will see and fear,
    and put their trust in the LORD.

PSALM 40:1,3

It will be said on that day,
    Lo, this is our God; we have waited for him, so
    that he might save us.
    This is the LORD for whom we have waited;
    let us be glad and rejoice in his salvation.

ISAIAH 25:9

Beloved, while you are waiting for these things, strive to be found by him at peace, without spot or blemish; and regard the patience of our Lord as salvation.

2 PETER 3:14–15

*W*aiting is hard. Our whole life is spent, one way or another, in waiting. Life is a series of hopes, and waitings, and half-fulfillments. We equate waiting with wasting. So we build Concorde airplanes, drink instant coffee, roll out green plastic and call it turf, and reach for the phone before we reach for the pen. The more life asks us to wait, the more we anxiously hurry. The tempo of haste in which we live has less to do with being on time or the efficiency of a busy life—it has more to do with our being unable to wait.

But waiting is unpractical time, good for nothing but mysteriously necessary to all that is becoming. As in a pregnancy, nothing of value comes into being without a period of quiet incubation; not a healthy baby, not a loving relationship, not a reconciliation, a new understanding, a work of art, never a transformation. Rather, a shortened period of incubation brings forth what is not whole or strong or even alive.

Brewing, baking, simmering, fermenting, ripening, germinating, gestating are the feminine processes of becoming, and they are the symbolic states of being which belong in a life of value, necessary to transformation.

Gertrud Mueller Nelson

Wisdom

Wise warriors are mightier than strong ones,
and those who have knowledge than those who
have strength.

PROVERBS 24:5

If you love to listen you will gain knowledge,
and if you pay attention you will become wise.

SIRACH 6:33

If any of you is lacking in wisdom, ask God, who gives to all generously and ungrudgingly, and it will be given you.

JAMES 1:5

The LORD gives wisdom;
from his mouth come knowledge and understanding;
he stores up sound wisdom for the upright;
he is a shield to those who walk blamelessly.

PROVERBS 2:6–7

Wisdom becomes known through speech, and education through the words of the tongue.

SIRACH 4:24

Jesus said, "Everyone then who hears these words of mine and acts on them will be like a wise man who built his house on rock. The rain fell, the floods came, and the winds blew and beat on that house, but it did not fall, because it had been founded on rock."

MATTHEW 7:24–25

Wisdom

Seek advice from every wise person and do not despise any useful counsel.

TOBIT 4:18

Get wisdom, get insight; do not forget, nor turn away
from the words of my mouth.
Do not forsake her, and she will keep you;
love her and she will guard you.
The beginning of wisdom is this: Get wisdom,
and whatever else you get, get insight.

PROVERBS 4:5–7

The fear of the LORD is the beginning of wisdom;
all those who practice it have a good understanding.

PSALM 111:10

With God are wisdom and strength;
he has counsel and understanding.

JOB 12:13

*I pray that the God of our Lord Jesus Christ, the
Father of glory, may give you a spirit of wisdom and
revelation as you come to know him.*

EPHESIANS 1:17

The quiet words of the wise are more to be heeded
than the shouting of a ruler among fools.
Wisdom is better than weapons of war,
but one bungler destroys much good.

ECCLESIASTES 9:17–18

Wisdom

My child, be attentive to my wisdom;
    incline your ear to my understanding,
so that you may hold on to prudence,
    and your lips may guard knowledge.

PROVERBS 5:1–2

Wisdom is as good as an inheritance,
    an advantage to those who see the sun.
For the protection of wisdom is like the protection of
money,
    and the advantage of knowledge is that wisdom
    gives life
to the one who possesses it.

ECCLESIASTES 7:11–12

God said to humankind,
"Truly, the fear of the Lord, that is wisdom,
    and to depart from evil is understanding."

JOB 28:28

Whoever walks with the wise becomes wise,
but the companion of fools suffers harm.

PROVERBS 13:20

May God grant me to speak with judgment,
and to have thoughts worthy of what I have received;
for he is the guide even of wisdom
and the corrector of the wise.

THE WISDOM OF SOLOMON 7:15

*W*isdom

Oh, how I love your law!
　　It is my meditation all day long.
Your commandment makes me wiser than my enemies,
　　for it is always with me.

PSALM 119:97–98

When you turn to the right or when you turn to the
left, your ears shall hear a word behind you, saying,
"This is the way; walk in it."

ISAIAH 30:21

Daniel said:
"Blessed be the name of God from age to age,
　　for wisdom and power are his.
He changes times and seasons,
　　deposes kings and sets up kings;
he gives wisdom to the wise
　　and knowledge to those who have understanding.
He reveals deep and hidden things;
　　he knows what is in the darkness,
　　and light dwells with him.
To you, O God of my ancestors,
　　I give thanks and praise,
for you have given me wisdom and power,
　　and have now revealed to me what we asked of you.

DANIEL 2:20–23

Wisdom

Doing wrong is like sport to a fool,
> but wise conduct is pleasure to a person of
> understanding.

PROVERBS 10:23

The mouths of the righteous utter wisdom,
> and their tongues speak justice.
The law of their God is in their hearts;
> their steps do not slip.

PSALM 37:30–31

Teach us to count our days
> that we may gain a wise heart.

PSALM 90:12

To the one who pleases him God gives wisdom and
knowledge and joy; but to the sinner he gives the work
for gathering and reaping, only to give to one who
pleases God.

ECCLESIASTES 2:26

Those who are wise shall shine like the brightness of
the sky and those who lead many to righteousness,
like the stars forever and ever.

DANIEL 12:3

Children and the building of a city establish one's name,
> but better than either is the one who finds wisdom.

SIRACH 40:19

*O*ne day, I was at work helping a patient prepare for her examination by the doctor. She was relating to me all her different problems. As we talked, I tried to point out to her certain things about her concerns. At the end of the conversation, she said to me, "Thank you for all the wisdom you have shared."

I said, "Wisdom? I don't know that I gave you any wisdom. In fact, I'm always praying for wisdom, but I am not sure that I have any." She said, "I would have you know that in the last twenty minutes when you spoke to me, all I heard was wisdom."

I left the room laughing, but perplexed. I said to the Lord, "Jesus, I've prayed so much for wisdom, and I don't know that I have it."

Immediately, in my spirit, I heard the Lord come right back: "I am Wisdom! Wisdom is not something that you acquire and carry around on your back. No, I am the source of all wisdom, and when you are in me and I am in you, I release it to you moment by moment as you need it. I give you my wisdom so you may be able to deal with things wisely."

Babsie Bleasdell

*W*itnessing

Peter and John answered them, ... "We cannot keep from speaking about what we have seen and heard."

ACTS 4:19–20

Awesome is the Lord and very great,
and marvelous is his power.
Glorify the Lord and exalt him as much as you can,
for he surpasses even that.
When you exalt him, summon all your strength,
and do not grow weary, for you cannot praise
him enough.

SIRACH 43:29–30

Jesus said, "Those who do what is true come to the light, so that it may be clearly seen that their deeds have been done in God."

JOHN 3:21

Jesus said, "You are the light of the world. A city built on a hill cannot be hid. No one after lighting a lamp puts it under the bushel basket, but on the lampstand, and it gives light to all in the house. In the same way, let your light shine before others, so that they may see your good works and give glory to your Father in heaven."

MATTHEW 5:14–16

*W*itnessing

If you confess with your lips that Jesus is Lord and believe in your heart that God raised him from the dead, you will be saved. For one believes with the heart and so is justified, and one confess with the mouth and so is saved.

ROMANS 10:9–10

Arise, shine; for your light has come,
and the glory of the LORD has risen upon you.

ISAIAH 60:1

Jesus said, "You will receive power when the Holy Spirit has come upon you; and you will be my witnesses in Jerusalem, in all Judea and Samaria, and to the ends of the earth."

ACTS 1:8

Jesus said, "Everyone therefore who acknowledges me before others, I also will acknowledge before my Father in heaven."

MATTHEW 10:32

You are my witnesses, says the LORD,
and my servant whom I have chosen,
so that you may know and believe me
and understand that I am he.
Before me no god was formed,
nor shall there be any after me.

ISAIAH 43:10

··

*W*itnessing

Jesus said, "Go therefore and make disciples of all nations, baptizing them in the name of the Father and of the Son and of the Holy Spirit, and teaching them to obey everything that I have commanded you. And remember, I am with you always, to the end of the age."

MATTHEW 28:19–20

In your hearts sanctify Christ as Lord. Always be ready to make your defense to anyone who demands from you an accounting for the hope that is in you.

1 PETER 3:15

God abides in those who confess that Jesus is the Son of God, and they abide in God.

1 JOHN 4:15

Do not fear, or be afraid;
> have I not told you from of old and declared it?
> You are my witnesses!

ISAIAH 44:8

Jesus said, "This good news of the kingdom will be proclaimed throughout the world as a testimony to all the nations."

MATTHEW 24:14

Jesus said, "I tell you, everyone who acknowledges me before others, the Son of Man also will acknowledge before the angels of God."

LUKE 12:8

··

J loathe squash. I don't care if you put brown sugar and butter on it. As far as I'm concerned, it's a repulsive gag-in-the-back–of-the-throat vegetable. As a result of my hostility toward squash, my son is not regularly exposed to it. (Let's be honest: He's never exposed to it.) In somewhat the same way, if we do not expose our children to our faith on a regular basis, we can't expect them to find any value in it.

Research by the Search Institute, an organization that examines religious issues as they pertain to youth, indicates that of all the factors leading to a mature acceptance of religion, parents and family top the list. Parents are more important than religion classes, Mass, friends, homilies, or priests. The Institute cites three key elements that make a definite difference in the transference of beliefs: talking about your faith; letting your kids see you practice your convictions by Mass attendance, daily prayer, and Scripture reading; and taking time to live your beliefs through service to others.

It comes down to a simple truth: If we want our children to have faith, we must practice our own. We cannot expect our children to embrace that which we ourselves do not value, be it squash or religion.

Woodene Koenig-Bricker

Work

Excel in all that you do;
> bring no stain upon your honor.

SIRACH 33:23

Six days you shall labor and do all your work. But the seventh day is a Sabbath to the LORD your God; you shall not do any work—you, or your son or your daughter, or your male or female slave, or your ox or your donkey, or any of your livestock, or the resident alien in your towns, so that your male and female slaves may rest as well as you.

DEUTERONOMY 5:13–14

From the fruit of the mouth one is filled with good things,
> and manual labor has its reward.

PROVERBS 12:14

Whatever your task, put yourselves into it, as done for the Lord and not for your masters since you know that from the Lord you will receive the inheritance as your reward; you serve the Lord Christ.

COLOSSIANS 3:23

A slack hand causes poverty,
> but the hand of the diligent makes rich.

PROVERBS 10:4

Work

All must test their own work; then that work, rather than their neighbor's work, will become a cause for pride. For all must carry their own loads.

GALATIANS 6:4–5

Whatever your hand finds to do, do with your might.

ECCLESIASTES 9:10

Stand by your agreement and attend to it,
    and grow old in your work.
Do not wonder at the works of a sinner,
    but trust in the Lord and keep at your job;
for it is easy in the sight of the Lord
    to make the poor rich suddenly, in an instant.

SIRACH 11:20–21

In the morning sow your seed, and at evening do not let your hands be idle; for you do not know which will prosper, this or that, or whether both alike will be good.

ECCLESIASTES 11:6

Wealth hastily gotten will dwindle,
    but those who gather little by little will increase it.

PROVERBS 13:11

Let the favor of the Lord our God be upon us,
    and prosper for us the work of our hands—
    O prosper the work of our hands!

PSALM 90:17

Work

To one who works, wages are not reckoned as a gift but as something due.

ROMANS 4:4

My beloved, be steadfast, immovable, always excelling in the work of the Lord, because you know that in the Lord your labor is not in vain.

1 CORINTHIANS 15:58

Whatever you do, in word or deed, do everything in the name of the Lord Jesus, giving thanks to God the Father through him.

COLOSSIANS 3:17

In all toil there is profit,
> but mere talk leads only to poverty.

PROVERBS 14:23

The appetite of workers works for them;
> their hunger urges them on.

PROVERBS 16:26

We urge you, beloved, to do so more and more, to aspire to live quietly, to mind your own affairs, and to work with your hands, as we directed you, so that you may behave properly toward outsiders and be dependent on no one.

1 THESSALONIANS 4:10–12

Work

Jesus said, "The one who had received the five talents came forward, bringing five more talents, saying, 'Master, you handed over to me five talents; see, I have made five more talents.' His master said to him, 'Well done, good and trustworthy slave; you have been trustworthy in a few things, I will put you in charge of many things; enter into the joy of your master.'"

MATTHEW 25:20–21

Jesus said, "Do not work for the food that perishes, but for the food that endures for eternal life, which the Son of Man will give you. For it is on him that God the Father has set his seal."

JOHN 6:27

The plans of the diligent lead surely to abundance,
    but everyone who is hasty comes only to want.

PROVERBS 21:5

Happy is everyone who fears the LORD,
    who walks in his ways.
Your shall eat the fruit of the labor of your hands;
    you shall be happy, and it shall go well with you.

PSALM 128:1–2

Jesus said, "Very truly, I tell you, the one who believes in me will also do the works that I do and, in fact, will do greater works than these, because I am going to the Father."

JOHN 14:12

Work

The one who plants and the one who waters have a common purpose, and each will receive wages according to the labor of each. For we are God's servants, working together; you are God's field, God's building.

1 Corinthians 3:8–9

Even when we were with you, we gave you this command: Anyone unwilling to work should not eat. For we hear that some of you are living in idleness, mere busybodies, not doing any work. Now such persons we command and exhort in the Lord Jesus Christ to do their work quietly and to earn their own living.

2 Thessalonians 3:10–12

God is not unjust; he will not overlook your work and the love that you showed for his sake in serving the saints, as you still do.

Hebrews 6:10

Do you see those who are skillful in their work?
   They will serve kings;
      they will not serve common people.

Proverbs 22:29

*A*fter I became a Christian I wished for a less worldly career: I wondered why God had not called me to some visibly Christian occupation.

Far from choosing his will, I was using my own daydreams about holiness as a way of resisting his will. In fact, I was resisting the less conspicuous call to be good in the work I already had. Following the opinion of the world, I doubted whether I could be holy unless I was engaged in some work that the world calls holy. It was some time before I came upon that quotation from Newman, "I shall be a preacher of truth in my own place"; still longer before I could accept or understand it. And the statement of Dorothy Sayers hit me very hard: "The only Christian work is good work well done."

As Christians we are called not only to be converted but also to convert the world. It was difficult for me sometimes to see that I could convert the world by remaining with it rather than by departing from it. I needed to learn, as Merton did after conversion, that the world we wish to be freed from is not "out there" but "in here."

Emilie Griffin

Worship

I will sing to my God a new song;
O Lord, you are great and glorious,
wonderful in strength, invincible.

JUDITH 16:13

All the angels ... worshiped God, singing,
"Amen! Blessing and glory and wisdom
and thanksgiving and honor
and power and might
be to our God forever and ever!
Amen."

REVELATION 7:11–12

*Through him, then, let us continually offer a sacrifice
of praise to God, that is, the fruit of lips that confess
his name.*

HEBREWS 13:15

You are worthy, our Lord and God,
to receive glory and honor and power,
for you created all things,
and by your will they existed and were created.

REVELATION 4:11

From the throne came a voice saying,
"Praise our God,
all you his servants,
and all who fear him,
small and great."

REVELATION 19:5

Worship

Make a joyful noise to the LORD, all the earth.
Worship the LORD with gladness;
come into his presence with singing.

PSALM 100:1–2

I will extol you, my God and King,
and bless your name forever and ever.
Every day I will bless you,
and praise your name forever and ever.
Great is the LORD, and greatly to be praised;
his greatness is unsearchable.

PSALM 145:1–3

O come, let us worship and bow down,
let us kneel before the LORD, our Maker!
For he is our God,
and we are the people of his pasture,
and the sheep of his hand.

PSALM 95:6–7

It is good to give thanks to the LORD,
to sing praises to your name, O Most High;
to declare your steadfast love in the morning,
and your faithfulness by night,
to the music of the lute and the harp
to the melody of the lyre.
For you, O LORD, have made me glad by your work;
at the works of your hands I sing for joy.

PSALM 92:1–4

ωorship

Be generous when you worship the Lord,
and do not stint the first fruits of your hands.

SIRACH 35:10

*Jesus said, "The hour is coming, and is now here,
when the true worshipers will worship the Father in
spirit and truth, for the Father seeks such as these to
worship him. God is spirit, and those who worship
him must worship in spirit and truth."*

JOHN 4:23–24

Worship the LORD in holy splendor;
tremble before him, all the earth.

PSALM 96:9

I will give thanks to the LORD with my whole heart;
I will tell of all your wonderful deeds.
I will be glad and exult in you;
I will sing praise to your name, O Most High.

PSALM 9:1–2

You shall worship the LORD your God.

EXODUS 23:25

*Jesus answered him, "It is written, 'Worship the Lord
your God, and serve only him.'"*

LUKE 4:8

Singing on life's pilgrimage can sustain you and give you new heart. Psalms and hymns can renew your energy for the way ahead, and help you to "lift your drooping hands and strengthen your weak knees" (Hebrews 12:12). They also help keep your vision focused on your destination. An Advent responsory in the Liturgy of the Hours describes this well: "We are Christ's pilgrim people, journeying until we reach our homeland, singing on the way as we eagerly expect the fulfillment of our hope, for if one hopes, even though his tongue is still, he is singing always in his heart."

While most of us know that singing hymns and psalms at Mass brings us more consciously into the presence of God and aids our worship, probably only a few of us make a practice of singing in our own times of personal prayer. When I began to sing some of my favorite songs during my morning prayer at home or while driving to work, my spiritual life was revived. Why not try it yourself?

Choose hymns and songs whose words reflect and express to the Lord what is in your heart, as well as ones that help you to praise him. And don't worry if you can't carry a tune— you are singing for God's ears only and he loves to listen to you! As Saint Augustine wrote, "He who sings prays twice."

Jeanne Kun

Sources

Page 9: Taken from *Dorothy Day. Selected Writings* edited by Robert Ellsberg. Copyright ©1983,1992 by Robert Ellsbert and Tamar Hennessey. Published in 1992 by Orbis Books, Maryknoll, New York 10545.

Page 15: Taken from *Walking on Water* by Madeleine L'Engle. Copyright ©1991 by Harold Shaw Publishers.

Page 21: Taken from *Dreams and Miracles* by Ann Spangler. Copyright©1997 by Ann Spangler. Used by permission of Zondervan.

Page 25: Taken from *How to Read and Pray the Parables* by Marilyn Gustin. Copyright ©1992 by Ligouri Publications. A Redemptorist publications can be used with permission of Ligouri Publications, Ligouri, MO 63057-9999. No other reproduction of this material is permitted.

Page 35: Copyright©1998 by Kathleen Spears Hopkins

Page 41: Taken from *Be Not Solicitous* by Maisie Ward. Copyright ©1953 by Sheed & Ward. All rights reserved.

Page 45: Taken from *Graham Cracker, Galoshes and God* by Bernadette McCarver Snyder. Copyright ©1995 by Ligouri Publications. A Redemptorist publications can be used with permission of Ligouri Publications, Ligouri, MO 63057-9999. No other reproduction of this material is permitted.

Page 51: Taken from *New Covenant Magazine* (October 1984). Copyright © by Sister Ann Shields. Used by permission of the author.

Page 57: Taken from *Dorothy Day: Selected Writings* edited by Robert Ellsberg. Copyright ©1983, 1992 by Robert Ellsbert and Tamar Hennessey. Published in 1992 by Orbis Books, Maryknoll, New York 10545.

Sources

Page 61: Taken from *An Angel a Day* by Ann Spangler. Copyright ©1994 by Ann Spangler. Used by permission of Zondervan.

Page 65: Copyright ©1998 by Carol Gura. Reprinted by permission of Thomas More Publishing. 200 East Bethany Drive, Allen, Texas 75002. All rights reserved.

Page 71: Taken from *Miracles Do Happen*. Copyright ©1987 by Briege McKenna and Henry Libersat. Published by Servant Publications, Box 8617, Ann Arbor, Michigan, 48107. Used by permission.

Page 75: Taken from *All Earth is Crammed with Heaven: Daily Reflections for Mothers* by Mary van Balen Holt. Copyright ©1996, Servant Publications. Used by permission of the author.

Page 79: Taken from "The Apples in a Seed" by Wendy Leifield. *New Covenant Magazine* (October 1994).

Page 83: Taken from *Enfolded in Love. Daily Readings with Julian of Norwich* by Julian of Norwich. Copyright © 1980 by Darton, Longma and Todd. LTD., London, England.

Page 87: Taken from *St. Chantal on Prayer* by Rev. A. Durand. Used by permission.

Page 91: Taken from *May They All Be One* by Chiara Lubich. Copyright © 1968, 1990 by New City Press. Used by permission of the publisher.

Page 97: Taken from *My Life Is in Your Hands* by Kathy Troccoli. Copyright © by Kathy Troccoli. Used by permission of Zondervan.

Page 101: Taken from *A Life-giving Way* by Esther De Waal. Copyright ©1995 by Liturgical Press. Used by permission.

Sources

Page 105: Taken from *Miracles Do Happen* by Briege McKenna and Henry Libersat. Copyright ©1987 by Briege McKenna and Henry Libersat. Published by Servant Publications, Box 8617, Ann Arbor, Michigan 48107. Used by permission.

Page 111: Copyright ©1998 by Carol Gura. Used by permission of the publisher, Thomas More Publishing, 200 East Bethany Drive, Allen, Texas 75002. All rights reserved.

Page 115: Taken from *No Greater Love* by Mother Teresa. Copyright ©1997. Used by permission of New World Library, Novato, California 94949.

Page 121: taken from *Turning, Reflections on the Experience of Conversion* by Emilie Griffin. Copyright ©1980 by Doubleday.

Page 127: Taken from *Mother Teresa, Contemplative in the Heart of the World* by Brother Angelo Devanda Scolozzi. Copyright ©1985 by Servant Books.

Page 135: Taken from *"Quality of Mercy."* New Covenant Magazine (June 1985). Used by permission of the author.

Page 141: Reprinted with permission from *God's Word Today*, Mystic, CT, July 1998. © Bayard Publications.

Page 147: Taken from *Seasons of Your Heart* by Marcrina Wiederkehr. Copyright ©1991 by Harper San Francisco.

Page 151: Taken from *From Union Square to Rome* by Dorothy Day. Copyright ©1978. Used by permission.

Page 157: Taken from *Balancing Act* by Mary Ellen Ashcroft. Copyright ©1996 by Mary Ellen Ashcroft. Used by permission of InterVarsity Press, P.O. Box 1400, Downers Grove, Illinois 60515.

Sources

Page 163: Taken from *Through Him, With Him, In Him* by Ruth Burrows. Copyright ©1987 by Dimension Books Inc. Denville, New Jersey 07834. Used by permission.

Page 169: Taken from *The Bible Today* [January 1986]. Published by the Liturgical Press. Copyright ©1986 by Irene Nowell, O.S.B. Used by permission of the author.

Page 173: Taken from *Miracles Do Happen*. Copyright ©1987 by Briege McKenna and Henry Libersat. Published by Servant Publications, Box 8617, Ann Arbor, Michigan, 48107. Used by permission.

Page 179: Taken from *The Comforting of Christ* by Caryll Houselander. Copyright ©1947 by Sheed & Ward. All rights reserved.

Page 183: Excerpt from *To Dance with God* by Gertrud Mueller Nelson. Copyright ©1986 by Gertrud Mueller Nelson, Paulist Press Inc., New York/Mahwah, N.J. Used by permission. www.paulistpress.com

Page 189: Taken from *Refresh Your Life in the Spirit*. Copyright ©1997 by Babsie Bleasdell with Henry Libersat. Published by Servant Publications, Box 8617, Ann Arbor, Michigan, 48017. Used by permission.

Page 193: Taken from *U.S. Catholic* magazine. Published by Claretian Publications.

Page 199: Taken from *To Believe in Jesus* by Ruth Burrows. Copyright ©1981,1978 by Dimension Books, Inc., Denville, New Jersey 07834. Used by permission.

Page 203: Taken from *God's Word Today* (December 1998). Used by permission of the author.

At Inspirio we love to hear from you—
your stories, your feedback,
and your product ideas.
Please send your comments to us
by way of e-mail at
icares@zondervan.com
or to the address below:

inspirio

Attn: Inspirio Cares
5300 Patterson Avenue SE
Grand Rapids, MI 49530

If you would like further information
about Inspirio and the products we
create please visit us at:
www.inspiriogifts.com

Thank you and God Bless!